T0319054

Cambridge Elements ☰

Elements in the Economics of Emerging Markets
edited by
Bruno S. Sergi
Harvard University

BANKING STABILITY AND FINANCIAL CONGLOMERATES IN EUROPEAN EMERGING COUNTRIES

Pavla Klepková Vodová
Silesian University in Opava

Iveta Palečková
Silesian University in Opava

Daniel Stavárek
Silesian University in Opava

CAMBRIDGE
UNIVERSITY PRESS

Shaftesbury Road, Cambridge CB2 8EA, United Kingdom

One Liberty Plaza, 20th Floor, New York, NY 10006, USA

477 Williamstown Road, Port Melbourne, VIC 3207, Australia

314–321, 3rd Floor, Plot 3, Splendor Forum, Jasola District Centre,
New Delhi – 110025, India

103 Penang Road, #05–06/07, Visioncrest Commercial, Singapore 238467

Cambridge University Press is part of Cambridge University Press & Assessment,
a department of the University of Cambridge.

We share the University's mission to contribute to society through the pursuit of
education, learning and research at the highest international levels of excellence.

www.cambridge.org
Information on this title: www.cambridge.org/9781009095112

DOI: 10.1017/9781009092166

First published 2022

A catalogue record for this publication is available from the British Library.

ISBN 978-1-009-09511-2 Paperback
ISSN 2631-8598 (online)
ISSN 2631-858X (print)

Cambridge University Press & Assessment has no responsibility for the persistence
or accuracy of URLs for external or third-party internet websites referred to in this
publication and does not guarantee that any content on such websites is, or will
remain, accurate or appropriate.

Banking Stability and Financial Conglomerates in European Emerging Countries

Elements in the Economics of Emerging Markets

DOI: 10.1017/9781009092166
First published online: December 2022

Pavla Klepková Vodová
Silesian University in Opava

Iveta Palečková
Silesian University in Opava

Daniel Stavárek
Silesian University in Opava

Author for correspondence: Pavla Klepková Vodová, klepkova@opf.slu.cz

Abstract: This Element focuses on the specific role of financial conglomerates in managing banking and financial stability. The Element aims to estimate financial stability in Central and Eastern Europe using the constructed aggregate financial stability index, to incorporate the financial stability of the parent company into the index, and to assess the effect of the parent company on the financial stability of commercial banks and national financial sectors.

This Element also has a video abstract: www.Cambridge.org/Economics of Emerging Markets_Vodova_abstract

Keywords: banking stability index, performance, liquidity, solvency, asset quality

ISBNs: 9781009095112 (PB), 9781009092166 (OC)
ISSNs: 2631-8598 (online), 2631-858X (print)

Contents

1 Introduction

This Element focuses on the specific role of financial conglomerates (financial groups) in managing banking and financial stability. This issue is undoubtedly one of the most debated topics in contemporary financial economics and deserves further attention for several reasons. First, financial conglomerates engage in a broad range of complex financial transactions and operate in various markets. Financial conglomerates, hence, have become risk managers rather than straightforward intermediaries. As a consequence, financial conglomerates are large in size and complex to oversee. They can also seek the size to maximize potential government support in case of need. Second, the character of financial conglomerates often qualifies them to be considered as systematically important financial institutions that are specially treated in legislation, also within the European Union (EU). The importance of financial conglomerates is reflected also in the close and regular cooperation of the three European Supervisory Authorities (European Banking Authority, European Insurance and Occupational Pensions Authority, and European Securities and Markets Authority) in the area of supervision of financial conglomerates. Third, if the local bank is a systematically important institution on the national level, but the conglomerate to which the bank belongs is not systematically important on the global or EU level, the vulnerability of banking sectors can increase substantially. All of these aspects can substantially influence the financial stability of individual banks and the entire banking sector.

In examining the issue of financial conglomerates and financial stability, we focus on the region of Central and Eastern Europe (CEE). Maintaining financial stability in CEE countries is based on several fundamental characteristics of the national financial sectors. The financial sector in CEE countries is dominated by banks. Commercial banks are the leading financial intermediaries, and they manage most of the financial assets. Therefore, attention should be paid primarily to banking stability, which represents an essential and crucial part of financial stability in the CEE region. Moreover, the banking sectors in CEE countries are characterized by a large market share of foreign capital and a high level of concentration. Nevertheless, the increasing competition and pressure on increasing profit and new trends in banking may encourage banks to make riskier behaviour, making them more fragile. Additionally, the banking sectors in CEE countries have undergone several changes during the past decades that can affect their stability.

Financial stability is a situation where the financial system operates with no serious failures or undesirable impacts on the present and future development of the economy as a whole, while showing a high degree of resilience to shocks (CNB, 2021). Policymakers, regulators, and academics devote significant attention to banking stability, methods of its measuring, and analysis of its determinants. Bank stability is also important for depositors: according to König-Kersting et al. (2022), bank deposits are sensitive to perceived bank performance. Banks with strong fundamentals benefit from precise disclosure, but more solvent banks with weaker fundamentals benefit from less precise information disclosure. Bank health can transmit very easily to non-financial firms (Chodorow-Reich and Falato, 2022).

According to World Bank (2021), there are numerous methods for measuring banking stability, including: (i) FSIs presented by International Monetary Fund (IMF) (including capital adequacy, asset quality, earning and profitability, liquidity, and sensitivity to market risk); (ii) Z-score (which explicitly compares buffers with risk); (iii) Merton's model (which is used to ascertain a bank's ability to meet its obligations and gauge the possibility of default); and (iv) the KMV (Kealhofer Merton Vasicek) model (where the distance to default measures a bank's solvency risk and liquidity risk). The aggregated index of financial stability, applied in this Element, is also possible. The index can summarize complex and multidimensional realities into one number and thus assess easily the overall financial health of the bank or banking system and it may enable to capture also the link between financial health of a bank and its parent company. This may be especially important mainly in those countries where banking systems are dominated by foreign banks and banks that belong to international financial groups, such as in CEE countries. We could see the increasing interconnection between banks from different countries: many banks offer their services in the domestic country and also in other countries through their subsidiaries or branches. The financial health of such banks affects financial stability of financial systems in different countries (e.g., Calomiris et al. (2022) investigated transmission of bank distress through interbank connections). As a result of increasing size of banks and increasing role of financial groups, the systemic risk and the risk of financial contagion became very real topics, especially for policymakers and regulatory and supervisory bodies (as pointed by Hassan and Miah (2022), changes in banking sector legislation may help to avoid a potential crisis); moreover, supervision enforcement actions are associated with enhanced financial stability and the impact is even greater during financial crises (Berger et al., 2022).

Based on the previous arguments, the aim of the Element is threefold. First, to estimate financial stability in CEE using the constructed aggregate financial stability index for individual commercial banks. Second, to incorporate the financial stability of the parent company into the index. Third, to assess the effect of the parent company (financial conglomerate) on the financial stability of commercial banks and national financial sectors.

In spite of the fact that there exist a number of empirical studies which measure financial stability with an aggregate financial stability index focusing on the geographic area of CEE countries, such as Geršl and Heřmánek (2008) for the Czech banking sector, Laznia (2013) for Slovakia, Albulescu (2010) and Roman and Sargu (2013) for Romania, and Kočišová and Stavárek (2018) for the EU countries), we believe that an important gap still exists in the empirical literature. Individual studies use different financial ratios. However, to the best of our knowledge, there is no empirical study that would consider the fact that financial stability of banks operating within financial group may be affected also by the financial stability of the parent company and measured this impact directly with the use of the aggregate financial stability index. The impact of the affiliation with the parent company was evaluated only partly by Ashcraft (2008), who suggested that a bank affiliated with a multi-bank holding company was significantly safer than either stand-alone bank or a bank affiliated with one-bank holding company; Zhang (2019), who found that the establishment of financial holding company can improve the stability of the subsidiary; or Raykov and Silva-Buston (2020), who suggested that holding company banks were more stable than independent banks when affected by a negative shock.

Therefore, the uniqueness of this Element lies in how innovatively the influence of financial conglomerates on financial stability is addressed. We construct a new type of aggregated banking stability index that contains, besides other factors, the technical efficiency of banks and also captures the affiliation with a financial group. This approach outperforms conventional banking stability measures applied in the existing literature. The Element represents the first comprehensive study of this kind focused on the CEE region. The importance of our analysis stems from the fact that banking sectors in CEE countries are dominated by institutions largely owned by foreign banks and financial groups. Therefore, the vulnerability of the banking sector in the CEE countries can increase substantially, as the performance of local banks can be affected not only by local factors but also by the fact that multinational financial groups try to implement their own strategies. The global financial crisis changed the institutional framework of banking supervision as well as the business models of financial conglomerates. Another strongpoint of the Element is that the analysis is performed on a time span that allows the comparison of periods before and after the global financial crisis. Generally, the Element gives a very deep insight into banking stability in CEE countries, the consequences, and impacts of the affiliation with financial groups on the financial stability of commercial banks. Hence, the Element addresses and fills a significant gap in current theoretical and empirical research in the financial stability area.

The Element is structured as follows. Section 2 provides a theoretical background on the financial stability of banks: we define the financial stability of banks and the importance of the financial stability measures; then we focus on the development of measures of financial stability and the current knowledge in the area of interest.

Section 3 is devoted to the banking sectors and financial conglomerates in the CEE countries: we define the term 'financial conglomerate' and its various corporate structures; we describe the motives for conglomeration; we characterize the impact of the affiliation with the financial conglomerate on banks and banking sectors; and finally, the basic characteristics of banking sectors in the CEE countries are provided. Although we often use the term 'financial conglomerate', as this term is not defined in the legislative process in particular countries, we use it in the meaning of financial group. For the purpose of the empirical part of this Element, we use the terms 'financial conglomerate' and 'financial group' as synonyms. We take into consideration the following countries: Czechia, Slovakia, Hungary, Poland, Romania, Bulgaria, Croatia, Serbia, Bosnia and Herzegovina, and Slovenia. Regarding financial conglomerates (financial groups), we will consider the following institutions as appropriate: Erste Group, KBC Group, Raiffeisen Group, Société Générale Group, and UniCredit Group.

The construction of the aggregate index of financial stability and the description of the data used is the content of Section 4. Section 5 represents the empirical application of the aggregated index to banks in the CEE countries, including presentation of results, and discussion. The final section offers concluding remarks.

2 Financial Stability of Banks from a Theoretical Perspective

This section focuses on current knowledge about financial and banking stability. First, the importance of financial stability measures and the definition of financial stability of banks are described. The financial stability of the financial system is beyond the scope of this Element and will therefore not be discussed in further detail. It is followed by an explanation of the development of measures of financial stability. In the last part of this section, studies that investigated the banking stability in the CEE region are presented.

2.1 Theoretical Aspects of Financial Stability

The importance of assessing financial stability in countries in CEE has increased rapidly since the recent financial crisis. Moreover, Sargu and Roman (2013) mentioned that the financial crisis, through its severe implications on the financial systems and the real economy, underlines the major importance that the evaluation of banking sector soundness has for the identification of the weak points and vulnerable banks, as it is known that if the problems are identified late, the solutions for solving them are costlier, and the risk that the vulnerabilities will spread in the whole banking system is greater.

To be able to detect potential threats to financial stability and take appropriate macro prudential measures early on, policymakers not only need to monitor and assess financial stability, but also to project its likely future development (Jakubík and Slačík, 2013). In addition, a stable and healthy banking sector plays an important role in the proper functioning of the economy (Ivicic et al., 2008). Financial stability is paramount for economic growth, as most transactions in the real economy are made through the financial system. Furthermore, the stability of the banking sector is an important topic in the economic and social context, as the banking crisis can have substantial negative effects on economic output and social welfare (Huljak, 2015). The existence of a strong, solid, and stable banking sector represents an extremely important element for all participants in the economic environment, either depositors, investors, or entrepreneurs, especially in the case of the CEE countries, in which case the economy is financed overwhelmingly through this channel, namely the bank-based financial system (Sargu and Roman, 2013). In other words, a sound financial system reinforces trust in the system and prevents phenomena such as a run on banks, which can destabilize an economy. Therefore, bank stability becomes an important topic.

Financial instability and its effects on the economy can be very costly due to its contagion or spillover effects to other parts of the economy. In fact, it may lead to a financial crisis with adverse consequences for the economy. As Greenwood et al. (2022) found, the higher probability of entering a financial crisis is associated with a combination of rapid credit and asset price growth over the period of prior three years. Problems in financial systems not only disrupt financial intermediation, but can also undermine the effectiveness of monetary policy, exacerbate economic downturns, trigger capital flight and exchange rate pressures, and create large fiscal costs related to rescuing troubled financial institutions (IMF, 2021). Therefore, it is fundamental to have a sound and stable financial system to support the efficient allocation of resources and the distribution of risks throughout the economy. Consequently, one of the main goals of central banks is to promote and maintain monetary and financial stability as it contributes to a healthy economy and sustainable growth.

2.2 Definition of Financial Stability

There is no unified definition of financial stability or banking stability. Although in the literature numerous definitions of financial stability can be found, most of them have in common that financial stability is about the absence of system-wide episodes in which the financial system fails to function (crises). Financial stability is not easy to define or measure given the interdependence and the complex interactions of different elements of the financial system between themselves and with the real economy (Gadanecz and Jayaram, 2009). Financial stability is a broad concept that relates to different aspects of finance. On a micro level, it refers to the market structures and to financial institutions themselves. On a macro level, it also relates to the monetary stability and to the functioning of the payment system. Failures in supervision or in the payment system may lead to financial instability (Jakubík and Slačík, 2013). Mishkin (1990) defined financial stability as an efficient allocation of resources to run the financial system without significant disruption. Schinasi (2004) suggests the definition of financial stability from its different characteristics. Broadly, financial stability can be thought of in terms of the ability of the financial system: (a) to facilitate both efficient allocation of economic resources – both spatially and, especially, intertemporally – and the effectiveness of other economic processes (such as wealth accumulation, economic growth, and ultimately social prosperity); (b) to assess, price, allocate, and manage financial risks; and (c) to maintain its ability to perform these key functions – even when affected by external shocks or by a build-up of imbalances – primarily through self-corrective mechanisms (Schinasi, 2004). Financial stability represents the ability of the financial system to absorb shocks faced by the system. Strictly speaking, a financial system can be characterized as stable in the absence of excessive volatility, stress, or crises (Gadanecz and Jayaram, 2009).

Similarly, financial stability can be defined as a condition in which the financial system is capable of withstanding shocks and the unravelling of financial imbalances, thereby mitigating the likelihood of disruptions in the financial intermediation process that are severe enough to significantly impair the allocation of savings to profitable investment opportunities (ECB, 2007). Therefore, financial system stability in a broad sense means both the avoidance of financial institutions failing in large numbers and the avoidance of serious disruptions to the intermediation functions of the financial system (IMF, 2005).

Another fundamental component of the financial stability framework is the definition of financial stability analysis as the study of potential sources of systemic risk arising from the interlinkages between financial system vulner-abilities and potential shocks coming from different sectors of the economy, financial markets, and macroeconomic developments (interbank exposures to systematically important bank and the risk of cross-country interbank contagion was analysed, e.g., by Matousek and Rummel (2020)).

It is necessary to mention the Basel III framework. Basel III considers the dimensions of systemic risk, and the other purpose includes the strengthening of the financial system against shocks and the maintenance of its functioning in times of stress without emergency support from central banks and governments. Moreover, the Basel Committee introduced, for example, capital buffers, a maximum leverage ratio and capital surcharges on (global) systemically important banks or financial institutions (SIFIs) (Krug et al., 2015). The recent financial crisis has demonstrated that a failure of SIFIs could seriously damage the stability of the financial system. Clayton and Schaab (2022) studied the scope for international cooperation in macroprudential policies. The authors provided a unified framework to think about international bank regulations and suggested concrete insights with the potential to improve on the current policy stance.

The issue of financial stability is related to banking stability. Kočišová and Stavárek (2018) stated that financial stability is a by-product of the stability conditions that prevail in the banking system, financial markets, and the real economy; and among them, banking stability appears to be a vital ingredient for financial stability. As such, banking stability can be treated as a forerunner of financial stability in an economy. It is confirmed by Vesala et al. (2005), who stated that the analysis of the banking sector is a central component of a broader financial stability.

Lindgren and Folkerts-Landau (1998) defined a sound banking system as one in which most banks (those accounting for most of the system's assets and liabilities) are solvent and are likely to remain so. The likelihood of remaining solvent will depend, among other things, on banks being profitable, well managed, and sufficiently well capitalized to withstand adverse events. In a dynamic and competitive market economy, efficiency and profitability are linked and their interaction will indicate the prospects for future solvency. Inefficient banks will make losses and eventually become insolvent and illiquid. Undercapitalized banks, that is, those with low net worth, will be fragile in the sense of being more prone to collapse when faced with a destabilizing shock, such as a major policy change, a sharp asset price adjustment, financial sector liberalization, or a natural disaster. Lindgren and Folkerts-Landau (1998) added that banking systems may exhibit different degrees of vulnerability over time. They may be functioning poorly or may be working relatively well now but exhibit signs (e.g., low earnings or capitalization) of probable future problems or potential crises.

2.3 Measurement of Financial and Banking Stability

The first known source in which the financial stability was analysed is a study of Sprague (1910), where attention is paid to confidence-building measures and to the results of neglecting such a problem; the tools to achieve such confidence. The tools proposed are generally spontaneous in nature and opportunistic. In addition, Minsky (1977), based on Keynes' ideas, built the theory of instability on the assumption that every capitalist economy is inherently deeply unstable. According to this theory, financial crises are an innate and inevitable feature of the capitalist system. According to the model, events leading to financial crises begin with an inadequate or external shock to the economy. This approach offers analytical tools to understand financial crises as internal fundamentals of contemporary economies.

Measurement of bank stability often proves to be a difficult task. Therefore, the authors used different indicators of bank stability: non-performing loans (NPLs) ratio, value adjustment costs, or some binary indicator based on default threshold (Huljak, 2015). Zigraiova and Havranek (2016) confirmed that bank stability is often measured indirectly, that is, by considering individual or systemic banking distress, effectively the negative of stability. In this sense, the NPL ratio is often used as a fragility indicator. However, Beck (2008) added that the NPL ratio only covers credit risk and cannot be directly linked to the likelihood of bank failure. Furthermore, Kaffash et al. (2018) used three proxies for banking sector stability, including a measure of the probability of the bankruptcy, a measure of liquidity stability, and financial development stability, similar to the study of Čihák and Hesse (2008).

During the past century, researchers and central banks have developed many methods and techniques to address financial stability. Beaver (1966) and Altman (1968) defined the use of financial ratios to predict bankruptcy. Beaver (1966) is the first to attempt the use of financial ratios to predict bankruptcy, while Altman (1968) conducted a study that combined information from several financial ratios in a single prediction model (Altman's Z-score model). Boyd and Graham (1986) proposed the Z-score methods as a risk indicator, measuring the probability that a bank holding company will fail or go bankrupt. Subsequently, Boyd and Graham (1988) and Boyd et al. (1993) also employ the Z-score as an indicator of the probability of bankruptcy and investigate the risk effects of mergers of bank holding companies with non-bank financial firms.

The Z-score was developed as a model to determine the risk of failure of companies in the manufacturing industry and not to assess the financial per-formance of banks. However, the use of Z-score models in the banking industry showed inaccuracies of up to 70 per cent. Altman (1993) then revised the original model and introduced the four-variance model. The new model further improved the predictive ability of his original model. Altman (2000) repeatedly came up with several revisions of the model to make it more accessible to different economic environments and to advance the prediction accuracy data. In the literature exist several further modifications and empirical applications of the Z-score, for example, Mercieca et al. (2007) or Maishanu (2004), who extended Altman's Z-score model for banks, suggesting eight financial ratios for assessing a bank's financial health.

The Z-score includes banks' buffers (profits and capital) and risk, which is measured through standard deviation of returns on assets. This measure is calculated as the sum of the capital–asset ratio and the return on assets (ROA) divided by the standard deviation of the ROA. A high Z-score indicates a lower probability of insolvency and, thus, more stability (Degl'Innocenti et al., 2018). In other words, the Z-score indicates how many standard deviations in ROA a bank is away from insolvency and, by extension, from the likelihood of failure (Zigraiova and Havranek, 2016). The underlying idea is to capture the number of standard deviations by which returns have to diminish in order to deplete the equity of a bank (Fiordelisi and Mare, 2014). The Z-score enables an easy and direct way to interpret the financial soundness of a banking institution, underlining the ability of a bank to face risk with the capital and profit buffers that the banking institution has (Sargu and Roman, 2013).

In the empirical literature, the Z-score is an extensively used measure of bank stability (e.g., Boyd et al., 2006; Hesse and Čihák, 2007; Iannotta et al., 2007; Lepetit et al., 2008; Laeven and Levine, 2009; Čihák and Hesse, 2010; Demirgüc-Kunt and Huizinga, 2010; Beck et al., 2012; Borgioli et al., 2013; Sargu and Roman, 2013; Fiordelisi and Mare, 2014; Fu et al., 2014; Schaeck and Čihák, 2014; Huljak, 2015; Lepetit and Strobel, 2015; Goetz et al., 2016; Degl'Innocenti et al., 2018; Danisman and Tarazi, 2020; or Audi et al., 2021). Its popularity comes from the fact that it is directly related to the probability of a bank's insolvency, that is, the probability that the value of its assets decreases more than the value of debt. Karim et al. (2019) confirmed that researchers tend to use the Z-score as a measure of bank stability, which measures the distance from insolvency relative to volatility, profitability, and leverage. This is due to the simple and accurate measurement of bank stability.

Another group of approaches to assess banking stability or soundness are indicators based on the CAMEL model. CAMEL analysis (Capital adequacy, Asset quality, Management, Earnings, and Liquidity) was developed by bank regulatory agencies in the United States in 1979 to evaluate the soundness and safety of individual banks in the country. The CAMEL system was recommended by the Basel Committee of the Bank for International Settlements as an early warning mechanism for the assessment of the overall soundness of banks. In 1997, a sixth component was added to measure banks' sensitivity to market risk, thereby becoming CAMELS. It is an international bank supervisory rating system applied to banks using a detailed analysis of ratios from financial statements used by bank regulators to evaluate the overall performance of banks and determine their strengths and weaknesses (ICA, 2020).

In practice, this method has been used by the regulatory authorities as a bank supervision instrument (Gilbert et al., 2000; Hays et al., 2009). Similarly, in the empirical literature, the CAMELS approach has been employed to assess the stability of the banking sectors (Godlewski, 2005; Ginevičius and Podviezko, 2013; or Altan et al., 2014). Brossard et al. (2007) estimated bank stability of European banks using the CAMELS approach during the period 1991–2005. Also, Baltes and Rodean (2014) adopted the CAMEL approach to investigate the stability of commercial banks listed on the Bucharest Stock Exchange. Their results showed that credit risk is their point of vulnerability, having a negative influence on the indicators considered in the proposed CAMELS model.

In recent decades, more sophisticated methods have been used. The European Central Bank (ECB) and the IMF aimed to develop frameworks for financial stability analysis to be applied in an international setting and therefore produced sets of financial stability indicators, called macroprudential indicators (MPIs) and FSIs, respectively. The objective of the set of financial stability indicators is to provide users with a rough idea of the soundness of the financial sector (IMF, 2006). FSIs are indicators of the current financial health and soundness of the financial institutions in a country, and of their corporate and household counterparts. They include both aggregated individual institution data and indicators that are representative of the markets in which financial institutions operate. They focus on indicators of financial soundness directly relevant for the IMF of the IMF financial sector IMF (2019).

The methodology for the compilation of the FSIs is outlined in the IMF (2006). The Guide was significantly amended in July 2008. These amendments bring the ECB and IMF methodologies into much closer alignment with each other. The summary of thirty-nine financial health indicators is divided into two groups. The core FSI indicators relate to five key areas relevant to the risks of the banking business and are compatible with the CAMELS methodology to assess the soundness of individual financial institutions. The main objective of the FSIs is international comparability, that is, a consistent methodology.

In parallel with the work on the FSIs, a project within the European System of Central Banks was developed to produce a report on the stability of the EU banking sector. The ECB, in cooperation with national central banks and banking supervisory institutions, started working on a methodology and collection of MPIs to monitor the financial health of the banking sector. Compared to the IMF's financial health indicators, a similar motivation is evident, that is, to capture the evolution of risks in the financial and especially in the banking sector. However, there are important differences. Agresti et al. (2008) presented similarities and differences between these indicators. Briefly, the MPI set has a much larger number of indicators. From the overview of the areas and categories monitored, there is a desire to identify and measure a significant number of factors that affect the financial health of the European banking sector. Also, the origins of the ECB and IMF approaches to creating financial stability indicators are clearly distinct. Other differences can be seen in the frequency, where MPIs are annual, IMF and FSIs are quarterly, and MPIs are disaggregated by bank size, while IMF and FSIs are only at the aggregate level.

Furthermore, many central banks through their financial stability reports attempt to assess the risks to financial stability by focusing on several key indicators or stress indices. Because assessing financial stability is a complex process, the analytical framework for monitoring financial stability is centred on macroprudential surveillance and is complemented by the surveillance of financial markets, the analysis of macro-financial links, and the surveillance of macroeconomic conditions (IMF, 2005). Additionally, some central banks have constructed a composite indicator of financial stability based on FSI, for example, the ECB, the Czech National Bank (CNB), the National Bank of Hungary, and the Croatian National Bank, and others use an aggregate measure to reflect banking stability or fragility.

The CNB computes a banking stability index using a weighted average of sub-indicators of banking sector soundness, including capital adequacy, profitability, balance sheet liquidity, asset quality, credit, and currency risk. The constructed index of financial ratios is expressed in terms of the standard deviation from its historical average. Additionally, the CNB also computes composite indices of financial conditions to reflect liquidity and creditworthiness of non-financial companies. The ECB computes a composite indicator of financial market liquidity in the euro area. The ECB indicator combines several measures covering four different markets and three different dimensions of market liquidity (tightness, depth, and resilience) as well as liquidity premia. The National Bank of Hungary also calculates a liquidity index along these lines.

Since 2000, there have been gradual efforts to develop an aggregated indicator of banking stability. Moreover, Gospodarchuk and Amosova (2020) showed that the global financial crisis of 2008 exposed the disadvantages of the traditional banking regulation instruments – their inability to capture the accumulating systemic risks. The inadequacy and flaws of the models presented by financial institutions on financial stability were shown. Therefore, it accelerated efforts to develop a single aggregate measure that could indicate the degree of financial fragility or stress. Composite indicators are such combinations of individual variables that can be assigned benchmark or threshold values for the purposes of monitoring key sectors of the economy and serving as leading indicators of crises (Gadanecz and Jayaram, 2009). Additionally, composite quantitative measures of financial system stability that could signal these conditions are intuitively attractive, as they could enable policymakers and financial system participants to: (a) better monitor the degree of financial stability of the system, (b) anticipate the sources and causes of financial stress to the system, and (c) communicate more effectively the impact of such conditions (Gadanecz and Jayaram, 2009).

Some authors focused on building and applying an aggregate index for the evaluation of the stability of the banking sector (bank stability index). For example, the banking stability was analysed in studies of Geršl and Heřmánek (2008), Maudos (2012), Ginevičius and Podviezko (2013), Laznia (2013), Mishra et al. (2013), Petrovska and Mihajlovska (2013), Roman and Sargu (2013), Popovska (2014), Karanovic and Karanovic (2015), Kočišová (2015), and Kočišová and Stavárek (2015, 2018). A detailed description of the methods used in the works of these authors can be found in Kočišová and Stavárek (2015). Furthermore, Shijaku (2017) calculated a new composite index as a measure of bank stability conditions, which includes a wide set of information rather than focusing only on one aspect of risk. Shahzad et al. (2020) developed the bank stability index on the basis of three-dimensional loan loss provision, capital regulation standard, and profitability.

Understanding the accuracy of measures of bank soundness that are widely used in the empirical banking literature is an important theme. Therefore, Chiaramonte et al. (2015) examined whether the Z-score is an accurate tool to predict bank distress and found that specifications that use the natural logarithm of the Z-score show a good predictive power to identify banks in distress and the Z-score performs as well as the CAMELS variables. The authors concluded that during the financial crisis the accuracy of the Z-score and of the CAMELS variables marginally improves. Chiaramonte et al. (2016) concluded that Z-score is able to predict bank failures with the accuracy of on average 76 per cent, while adding a set of other bank- and macro-level variables can only marginally increase the model's predictability. In addition, Pietrzak (2021) showed that FSIs can be successfully used for macro-financial surveillance. The author claimed that using FSIs can be beneficial in conducting macro-financial surveillance as they can signal early enough tightness of financial conditions.

2.4 Review of the Literature on Banking Stability in the CEE

This section will present studies focused on the CEE banking sectors of the CEE or selected European countries where CEE countries are included. Most studies used the Z-score or the Banking Stability Index to measure banking stability. However, several studies have focused on the determinants of banking stability or studies focused on a link between banking stability and another economic aspect. This topic is not the subject of this Element, so it will not be addressed in detail.

Some researchers focused on the banking stability in the CEE. For example, Karkowska and Pawłowska (2017) used Z-score to analyse the bank stability of CEE countries. They estimated that the Hungarian, Czech, and Polish banks were more stable than Bulgarian, Slovenian, and the least stable were banks in Slovakia. Similarly, Lapteacru (2016) applied the Z-score in the CEE countries and found that the most stable were the banking sectors in Czechia, Slovakia, or Poland. On the other hand, the lowest stability using the Z-score was found in the banking sector of Romania, Slovenia, or Hungary. Furthermore, the stability measured by the Z-score decreased in the period 2007–8. Moreover, Bilan and Roman (2016) analysed the financial stability in CEE using the Z-score. Their results emphasized the importance of ensuring a healthy and sound macroeconomic environment for the financial health of banks. In addition, the authors highlight that the dynamics of bank credit in the private sector is the main risk factor for the soundness of the banking sector in CEE countries, which calls for its rigorous monitoring.

Several authors estimated the banking stability in individual CEE countries. For example, Geršl and Heřmánek (2008) developed banking stability index for Czechia using the FSI for deposit takers. That is, they used four indicators of capital adequacy, asset quality, earnings and profitability, liquidity, and exposure to foreign exchange risk. Šubová and Kočišová (2019) measured the stability of the Slovak banking using the Z-score and concluded that the Slovak banking sector was the most stable in Europe, but it has been influenced by significant changes, globalization, innovations, and deregulation. Furthermore, the Slovak banking sector was also influenced by the global financial crisis of 2008. Dumičić (2016) studied financial stability through the processes of accumulation and materialization of systemic risks in Croatia to facilitate the monitoring and understanding of the degree of financial stability and communication of macroprudential policymakers. The author found that the process of risk accumulation in Croatia was related to a strong lending activity to the greatest extent, while the materialization of systemic risks was revealed in the bank balance sheets as an increase in the NPL ratio. Moreover, Sargu and Roman (2013) used the CAMEL model to analyse

Romanian banks and found a quite heterogeneous distribution of the banks from the sample.

Kočišová (2015) applied the aggregate banking stability index for ten European countries that joined the EU in 2004. The result showed a decline in the average banking stability in the EU countries during the period 2005–8 and its improvement since 2009. Furthermore, Gulaliyev et al. (2019) analysed the banking sectors of twenty-nine countries using the composite financial stability index to build a risk map based on their national basic economic indicators. They ranked countries according to five levels of the banking system ('very high' or A, 'high' or B, 'acceptable' or C, 'low' or D, and 'very low' or E). The CEE banking sectors were classified as B–E. The most stable banking sector of the CEE countries was Czechia and Poland (B level); the lowest stable was Croatia (E level).

Some of the empirical studies on banking stability analysed European countries, where selected CEE countries were included. For example, Kočišová and Stavárek (2018) proposed a bank stability index to assess banking stability in EU countries during the period 2004–14. The authors found that during the period 2004–8, the average value of the indices decreased to its minimal values in 2008. It mirrored the negative effects of the financial crisis that hit the banking sectors in all EU countries. The gradual increase was found in the years 2008–14. The positive development in banking stability during this second stage was influenced mainly by the growing demand for increasing capital adequacy, which was related to the gradual implementation of Basel III. Another factor with positive impact was the growth of the liquidity component. Trends of the other components (asset quality, earnings, and profitability) can be considered stable. Moreover, Kočišová (2020) estimated the stability of the European Global Systematically Important Bank. Bank stability was measured by two proxies: Z-score and loan loss provisions. Her results show that the increasing share of fixed assets in total assets, the increase in bank liquidity, economic growth, and the measure of lagged stability had a positive impact on bank stability.

In the empirical literature, the authors have often focused on the impact of the financial crisis on bank stability. For example, Miklaszewska et al. (2012) used the Z-score bank stability index to measure bank stability in CEE-5 countries. The authors found a sharp decline in bank stability during the financial crisis, followed by an increase in the Z-score during 2009–10. This increase could be explained by the reinvestment over these two years. Furthermore, Capraru and Andries (2015) showed that during the period 2004–8, the Z-score continuously increased for seventeen countries in the CEE, which means an improvement in the financial stability of bank system. This can be explained by the process of harmonization of national regulatory framework with the acquis of the EU. The impact of the financial crisis on banking stability confirmed Jakubík and Slačík (2013), who estimated the bank stability using the financial instability index in CEE countries. The authors found that the economic crisis has, at least at some point, brought about elevated levels of financial stress in all countries under observation, except Slovakia. In all observed countries, the first two years of crisis years impaired financial stability more than the subsequent crises of sovereign debt and euro crises. In Poland, Bulgaria, and Romania, financial instability peaked in 2008, suggesting that the very first phase of the crisis was transmitted particularly through short-term channels such as stock or currency markets. On the contrary, in the remaining countries, financial stress reached the highest levels with a one-year lag in 2009, reflecting markets' uncertainty about longer-term fundamental and real economy issues (e.g., fiscal deficits, low growth), which took some time to penetrate some of the components of financial stability index. Furthermore, the authors indicated that credit growth combined with the level of credit to the private sector is a particularly good leading indicator of financial instability. Furthermore, they suggest that increasing credit risk and/or a high level of NPL stock reduces the capacity of the banking sector to support economic growth and thus imposes a significant risk to financial stability over a one-year period.

Brei et al. (2020) measured the degree of banking system stability by the Z-score (or distance to default) and found that the distance to default dropped during the financial crisis in advanced economies but varied somewhat less in emerging market economies. The authors covered thirty-two economies – fifteen advanced and seventeen emerging – and used annual data over the period 2007–15. Kim et al. (2020) explored the effect of bank diversification on financial stability using a sample of commercial banks based in OECD (Organisation for Economic Co-operation and Development) countries and concluded that during crisis periods, it is better for banks to concentrate on traditional intermediation functions rather than diversifying their activities and investments.

Several authors (e.g., Berger and Demirgüç-Kunt, 2021; Duan et al., 2021; and Park and Shin, 2021) started to study the new topic and indicated the impact of the Covid-19 pandemic on the financial stability. The preliminary research in this topic indicates that this crisis opens other issues in the financial stability. Didier et al. (2021) warned that the current regulatory infrastructure was not designed to deal with an exogenous systemic shock, such as the Covid-19 pandemic. They proposed that it could intensify the problem as it penalizes firms that face difficulties, leading to inefficient bankruptcies during the Covid-19 pandemic. As a result, policymakers face several challenges in reducing overall systemic risk. Ellis et al. (2021) suggested that the stress testing has also become an important new challenge in light of the Covid-19 pandemic.

This section merely outlines the most common findings of studies linking bank stability to other banking factors. For example, Huljak (2015) concluded that banking stability is the result of lower portfolio risk supporting the franchise value channel. The author concluded that for banks in CEE countries where the economic crisis increased the materialization of risk, increasing competition may have been a factor that decreased bank stability. Moreover, the author showed that during the period 2001–8, banks had a period of high credit growth accompanied with high loan portfolio quality, which resulted with stable and high earnings that brought their Z-score to historical maximum. However, he suggested the slight decrease in the banking stability measured using Z-score during 2008–11.

In addition, Alakbarov et al. (2018) proposed the banking stability index to estimate the financial stability of banking sectors in twenty-nine countries, including CEE banking sectors. The authors confirmed the thesis, according to which there are limits to the economic benefits from the creation of liquidity. These findings are in line with the results of Acharya and Naqvi (2012), who estimated that excess liquidity may lead to a deeper crisis for the banking sector. The resulting asset bubble potentially increases the vulnerability of the banking sector and increases the risks of generating a financial crisis. Furthermore, the authors concluded that liquidity risk is more important than credit risk in a downturn than during a boom. The CEE banking sectors are associated with a high share of foreign capital, which is why some studies have focused on examining the impact of foreign ownership on banking stability. Karkowska and Pawłowska (2017) found that the Z-score was negatively correlated with foreign ownership. Similarly, Wu et al. (2017) used the Z-score and investigated banks from thirty-five emerging economies, including countries in CEE, during the period 2000–14. They found that the risk of domestic banks increases with the penetration of foreign banks into the host economy. De Haas and Van Lelyveld (2006) considered whether foreign and domestic banks in CEE react differently to business cycles and banking crises. They found that during crisis periods, domestic banks contracted their credit base, whereas greenfield foreign banks did not. In addition, the conditions in the home country matter for the growth of foreign bank. Furthermore, the growth of credit from greenfield foreign banks is influenced by the health of the parent bank. In contrast, Dages et al. (2000) also found that domestically owned and foreign-owned banks with low problem loan ratios behave similarly, which suggests that bank health, and not ownership as such, has been critical.

In the empirical literature, financial stability is very often associated with the competition. Because it is not the subject of this Element, we only outline that the literature offers two opposing views: the paradigm of 'competition-fragility' (e.g., Agoraki et al., 2011; Leroy and Lucotte, 2017; Azmi et al., 2019; Ijaz et al., 2020) and the paradigm of 'competition stability' (e.g., Uhde and Heimeshoff, 2009; Fiordelisi and Mare, 2014; Schaeck and Čihák, 2014; Huljak, 2015; Shijaku, 2017; Clark et al., 2018; Ahi and Laidroo, 2019; Minh et al., 2020). The competition-fragility paradigm argues that high level of competition in the banking sector may lead to higher fragility of banks. Under this paradigm, banking competition can lower the interest income for banks and therefore, eroding banks' profits, which can lead to increased probability of default, and consequently, an overall disruption of the financial system. On the other hand, in a less competitive banking market, banks tend to do less aggressive operations and can create higher capital buffers, enhancing the stability of the whole banking sector.

3 Banking Sectors and Financial Conglomerates in CEE

The first part of this section defines the term 'financial conglomerate'. The second part focuses on the impact of the affiliation with the financial conglomerate on banks and banking sectors. After that, we will describe the banking sectors in CEE countries and characterize selected financial conglomerates operating in these banking sectors.

3.1 Theoretical Aspects of Financial Conglomerates

The emergence of financial conglomerates is one of the major trends in the financial sector in recent years. The term 'financial conglomerate' is defined differently in individual countries. Differences can be found especially while comparing its definition for the United States, the EU, and Japan (Supangkat et al., 2020). In the most general sense, a financial conglomerate is a group of entities whose primary business is financial and whose regulated entities engage to a significant extent in at least two of the activities of banking, insurance, and securities (Joint Forum, 1999). Given the purpose of this Element, we will pay attention only to the legislation in the EU. According to the Financial Conglomerates Directive (2002/87/EC), a financial conglomerate is a group which meets the following conditions:

- A regulated entity is at the head of the group or at least one of the subsidiaries in the group is a regulated entity.
- Where there is a regulated entity at the head of the group, it is either a parent undertaking of an entity in the financial sector, an entity which holds a participation in an entity in the financial sector, or an entity linked with an entity in the financial sector by a relationship.

– Where there is no regulated entity at the head of the group, the group's activities mainly occur in the financial sector.
– At least one of the entities in the group is within the insurance sector and at least one is within the banking or investment services sector.
– The consolidated and/or aggregated activities of the entities in the group within the insurance sector and the consolidated and/or aggregated activities of the entities within the banking and investment services sector are both significant.

A group is a set of undertakings, consisting foremost of a parent undertaking and its subsidiaries. The supervisory authorities can include in the group entities even if they do not formally meet the definition of parent subsidiary, if they identify the dominant influence. Moreover, the group also includes the participating interests held by the parent and subsidiaries. Finally, horizontal groups were equally covered (Dierick, 2004).

Primary motives for conglomeration are revenue enhancement and cost savings. Conglomeration is encouraged mainly by:

– improvements in information technology (it may significantly lower the operational costs per unit; large financial institutions are generally better able to finance extensive investments in information technology);
– globalization and consolidation of financial markets (which allows an unprecedented expansion of financial institutions);
– financial deregulation (which opens new markets and allows new cooperative links);
– expansion and diversifications;
– changes in demand for financial services (customers also change their requirements, they usually prefer to get more products in one place);
– financial institutions enter more diverse product markets (e.g., banks sell insurance products), offer innovative mixed products or use new distribution channels, their activities are becoming more complex, and so their organizational structures.

In regard to their structure, financial conglomerates may have different structures depending on legislation and traditions in individual countries. However, we can distinguish financial conglomerates according to the sector that is represented at the holding company level or by the type of activity of the major business of the financial conglomerate. For capital adequacy requirements, two types of financial conglomerates are defined:

– Insurance-led financial conglomerates.
– Banking-led or investment-led financial conglomerates (Commission Delegated Regulation No 342/2014).

Insurance-led financial conglomerate means a financial conglomerate with insurance as its most important financial sector. In that case, the parent or dominant group entity is an insurance company. A relatively small banking subsidiary is a part of such conglomerate. In the case of banking-led financial conglomerates or investment-led financial conglomerates, the most important financial sector is either the banking sector or the investment services sector. A banking-led financial conglomerate has a parent company in the form of a banking institution under supervision; smaller, less important subsidiaries include securities firms and/or insurance companies. In the case of investment-led financial conglomerates, the regulatory scheme is focused mainly on the regulated securities firm; subsidiaries from other financial sectors are less important (BIS, 1995).

Financial conglomerates can provide financial services through various corporate structures. We can distinguish four basic models:

- The integrated model
- The parent-subsidiary model
- The holding company model
- The horizontal group model (Dierick, 2004).

One and the same entity offers financial services in the integrated model. It corresponds to the universal bank model where the same bank provides commercial and investment banking. Maximum realization of the synergies and diversification between activities are the clear benefits of this model as a financial conglomerate can produce any given output at the lowest cost (due to neither legal nor operational separateness, it can exploit economies of scope). The potential conflict of interest, the potential risk of contagion, and the fact that banking businesses do not have to be insulated from the risks associated with other activities belong to risks of the integrated model.

The essence of the next three models is visible also from Figure 1. The parent-subsidiary model occurs relatively commonly in several possible forms: a bank as a parent company and an insurance undertaking as a subsidiary, or, conversely, an insurance undertaking as a parent company and a bank as a subsidiary. Therefore, it is a relationship between two or more companies, where one of them has a leading position as a parent company and establishes other companies as its subsidiaries (subsidiaries may be, e.g., funds or securities firms). The parent company has often a great influence on its subsidiaries. The legal separation between parent and subsidiary creates also operational separateness, which means that the synergy and diversification benefits of the integrated model cannot be fully realized. Both the parent and subsidiary must be separately capitalized. Moreover, there exists an agency problem. However, at

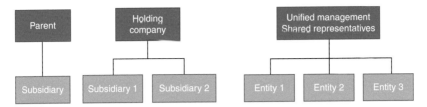

Figure 1 Selected models of corporate structure of financial conglomerates
Source: Authors' processing based on Dierick (2004), pp. 18–19.

least from a legal point of view, the parent company does not have to cover the liabilities of its subsidiaries (Dierick, 2004). Limited losses, the possibility to exploit tax benefits, and reduction of regulatory costs are other advantages of the parent-subsidiary model (Peleckiene et al., 2011).

The holding company model is headed by a company that does not carry out any special activities. Its task is to control specialized subsidiaries. In addition, the holding company is incharge of functions that are common to the entire group, such as risk management, raising and distributing capital, auditing, IT services, administration, training, and more. What is the main difference between the parent-subsidiary model and the holding company model? In case of the parent-subsidiary model, profits of the subsidiary accrue directly to the parent company. By contrast, the subsidiaries have no direct access to the profits or assets of the parent. The following are advantages of the holding company model: the management structure (i.e., the holding company is incharge of functions common for the whole group) takes better into account the know-how of all business areas, and it is easier to evaluate each company on a stand-alone basis. The possible risk of the holding company model arises in case of possible sale of individual subsidiaries, as they may not be capable of operating independently (due to the centralization of the previously mentioned functions).

The horizontal group model (the last part of Figure 1) is such a corporate structure where the entities are not linked to each other through direct or indirect capital links. Such groups are managed on a unified basis due to a contract or provision in the memorandum or articles of association. Therefore, it is relatively difficult to identify these groups and even more difficult to regulate them effectively.

In reality, the structure of individual financial groups is often more complex and mixtures of these models frequently occur in the same group. The structure of a financial conglomerate depends on the customs and practices in different countries, rules, and legislation and activities of banks involved in the conglomerate. Structure of the financial conglomerate is influenced mainly by the major field of business of its holding company. Mixing of commercial activities in financial conglomerates is the reason their supervision should be much more complex. Some conglomerates belong to the biggest financial groups, active in the international financial markets and providing services on a global basis. As the potential financial difficulties of such financial groups could seriously destabilize the financial system, it is evident that their financial stability is important also on a global basis. It is therefore not surprising that the legislation is also addressed at the supranational level. More detailed information about the corporate structure of international financial conglomerates and their possible preference of the absence of regulatory and tax distortions is analysed, for example, by Herring and Carmassi (2012).

Historically, financial groups have been supervised only within individual business lines. The need for a comprehensive perspective (in addition to sectoral supervision) as a condition for efficient financial group supervision was generally adopted during the 1990s. The comprehensive perspective allows supervisors to assess realistically the overall risks of the group and its capital coverage. The lack of a prudential framework for financial groups may hamper the effective supervision of these groups. Therefore, the Directive 2002/87/EC of the European Parliament and of the Council regarding regulatory technical standards specifying the definitions and coordinating the supplementary supervision of risk concentration and intragroup transaction (FICOD I – Financial Conglomerate Directive) was adopted in 2002. This directive introduces complementary pan-European supervision of financial groups, with the aim to increase financial stability and to protect creditors and depositors. The directive was amended in 2011: the Directive 2011/89/EU of the European Parliament and of the Council of 16 November 2011 amending Directives 98/78/EC, 2002/87/EC, 2006/48/EC and 2009/138/EC as regards the supplementary supervision of financial entities in a financial conglomerate (FICOD II). The aim of these directives is (i) to strengthen the role of supervisory authorities to ensure the capital adequacy of the regulated bodies; (ii) to prevent the use of the same capital by two or more members of the financial group; and (iii) to prevent the use of capital created within the financial group.

3.2 Impact of the Affiliation with the Financial Conglomerate on Banks and Banking Sectors

The affiliation with the financial conglomerate may have both a positive impact and a negative impact on financial stability. Financial groups usually show a high level of complementarity between products and services offered by different entities within the group, which brings them an economic advantage.

A financial group that combines different industry companies under one roof can use a wider distribution network and extensive infrastructure to achieve cost–benefit synergies across business lines. The combination of sector-specific financial services enables mutual marketing and cross-selling of products and services. It offers opportunities to expand the traditional products and services of institutions and customer base while strengthening a higher level of innovation in products and services. Moreover, the affiliation with financial conglomerates should increase bank efficiency. Information benefits that allow financial conglomerates to offer a wider set of relevant services for their clients through the reuse of relevant information about clients in different business sectors are the main source of higher operational efficiency. However, any increased efficiency can be offset by increased monopoly power if the growth of financial conglomerates reduces the number of firms operating in the banking and other financial sectors. A reduced competition in the market could in turn increase efficiency. The net effect of financial conglomerates on bank efficiency is therefore not clear.

Freixas et al. (2007) and Mälkönen (2009) concluded that financial conglomerates are financially more stable than stand-alone institutions. However, empirical evidence is scarce. According to our awareness, there are only a few studies that investigate the effect of affiliation with a financial conglomerate on individual aspects of financial stability. Vander Vennet (2002) found that European conglomerates were more revenue efficient than their specialized competitors. Palečková (2018) analysed the determinants of banking performance in banking sectors of CEE countries within the period 2005–15. She found that commercial banks in a financial conglomerate were, in average, more efficient and profitable than stand-alone commercial banks, even though the commercial banks in financial conglomerates reflected a lower average net interest income than other banks. Nevertheless, she did not conclude that all commercial banks in the financial conglomerate were more efficient and profitable than other banks in the banking sector. Therefore, she did not confirm the results of Vander Vennet (2002). Klepková Vodová (2019) investigated if the bank solvency is influenced by the affiliation of banks with financial conglomerates in six selected CEE countries within the period 2001–17. However, the results showed that the affiliation with financial conglomerates does not statistically significantly affect bank solvency; instead, some bank-specific and macroeconomic factors matter. Klepková Vodová (2018) also focused on the level of bank liquidity and solvency in the Visegrad countries within 2000–16. However, her results were mixed, so she could not confirm that banks belonging to financial conglomerates are more or less liquid and solvent than other banks in selected banking sectors.

Conglomeration leads to a diversification of risks (the diversification benefit, measured typically based on the conglomerate's economic capital relative to the sum of stand-alone capital) but, at the same time, to a decrease in shareholder value (the conglomerate discount, measured by a reduction of a firm value, caused by asymmetric information distribution) (Gatzert and Schmeiser, 2008).

Financial conglomerates can generally achieve a high degree of income and risk diversification due to the fact that they can divide their activities into different financial sectors. The expansion of risk and reduction of revenue fluctuations can, in turn, reduce the probability of financial distress and the need for external financing. The significant difference of banking, insurance, and investment activities and their risk profiles may encourage financial groups to realize the full potential of diversification benefits by engaging in cross-sectoral risk transfer sectors. Cross-sectoral risk transfers may be motivated by legal and tax considerations, accounting benefits, and possibility of advantage of regulatory arbitrage among different financial sectors. Financial groups usually diversify their financial activities to branches or subsidiaries around the world, which makes them less vulnerable to economical downturns in one country or region. Risk diversification is greater for international financial groups than for national ones (Berger et al., 2005). However, diversification can actually increase the income volatility of financial institutions (Staikouras and Wood, 2004). In addition, conglomerations generally lead to an increase in size and market capitalization, which improves the market position of the institution and discourages hostile takeover attempts.

Conglomeration leads also to information and knowledge benefits. Financial groups may offer a more diverse range of products than specialized financial institutions. Their level of information and monitoring costs is lower, as they can use information from basic bank account management to sell other financial products or services to the same customer. As a result, customers may benefit from better and cheaper financial services.

Within a financial conglomerate, it is possible to transfer know-how from one financial sector to another. Conglomeration increases market concentration and reduces competition. It enables to use capital arbitrage within a financial group, it means double or multiple transfers of capital. It is also possible to manage liquidity within the group, mainly with the use of intragroup lending.

However, financial conglomerates are linked not only with these benefits but also to a number of issues, particularly in terms of management autonomy, corporate transparency, and conflict of interest. Conglomeration may also exacerbate existing ones and create new financial and legal risks. The problems of financial conglomerates are mainly in different legislation, risk concentration, transparency, and the need for specific supervision. As pointed in Dierick (2004), financial conglomerates are connected with:

- higher risks arising from the possibility of regulatory arbitrage (regulatory arbitrage means double or multiple gearing (i.e., the same capital is used by two or more regulated entities within the group) or excessive leveraging, which occurs when debt is issued by a parent company and proceeded down in the form of equity to a regulated entity in the group),
- the risk of contagion within the group (which means that difficulties in one group entity may spill over to the other ones, either through economic links such as capital holdings, loans, guarantees, or indirectly through the behaviour of third parties such as customers or investors),
- moral hazard (first, there is a risk of the non-regulated entity in the group; second, the conglomerate may become so large that it is perceived as 'too big to fail' by market participants; third, group entities may expect help from other group entities in case of financial distress and so behave in a riskier way),
- lack of transparency for market participants and supervisors (due to the size and complexity of the financial group, it may be difficult to see accurately the structure of the group, its risk profile, and the essence of intragroup transactions),
- conflict of interest in different roles in customer dealing (the sharing of customer information within the group may violate privacy laws), and
- the possibility of abuse of economic power (financial conglomerates may increase market concentration, lower competition, as they are in a better position to fight competitors – and as a result, the incentives for innovation may be lower).

Moreover, Laeven and Levine (2007) found that markets assign lower values to financial conglomerates that engage in multiple activities than if those financial conglomerates were broken into financial intermediaries that specialized in the individual activities. The authors concluded that diversification reduces the value of financial conglomerates. One explanation of these results is that financial conglomerates that engage in multiple activities intensify agency problems and destroy value. Their results showed, however, that economies of scope in financial intermediation are not sufficiently large to compensate for countervailing forces associated with diversification since they consistently found a diversification discount, never a diversification premium.

Schmid and Walter (2009) focused on scope in financial intermediation and found that the impact of functional scope among financial intermediaries is predominantly value-destroying. The authors concluded that the negative elements present in financial conglomerates outweigh the positive elements, so that functional breadth impairs both competitive performance and shareholder value. This conglomerate discount applies in main financial activity-areas: credit intermediation, securities, and insurance.

The conflict of interest in different roles in customer dealing, and thus the activity of financial conglomerates, can be connected also with the use or abuse of private information. Massa and Rehman (2008) investigated how information flows within financial conglomerates affect behaviour of members of the same financial group. They found that mutual funds increase their stakes in the firms that borrow from their affiliated banks. Funds increase or decrease their stock holdings in those companies that subsequently provide positive or negative abnormal returns, suggesting that such behaviour is based on private information that are not available to other market participants.

The presence of international financial conglomerates in a banking sector opens the question if the current level of bankruptcy laws and procedures is efficient enough to resolve the bankruptcy adequately. Herring (2003) provides some examples and discuss possible risks and benefits of different approaches.

The existence of financial conglomerates influences also the level of efficiency of monetary policy. Campello (2002) found that if a small bank operates under a multi-bank holding company with another bank with easy access to funds, then its lending activity is not affected in periods of tight money. On the contrary, lending activity of small banks operating on a stand-alone basis becomes significantly more dependent on its own cash flows in periods of tightened monetary policy.

3.3 Banking Sectors in CEE Countries

As the research is focused on the region of CEE, it is useful to describe briefly the banking sectors in these countries. We will focus on banking sectors in Czechia (CZ), Slovakia (SK), Hungary (HU), Poland (PL), Romania (RO), Bulgaria (BG), Croatia (HR), Serbia (RS), Bosnia and Herzegovina (BA), and Slovenia (SL). These countries can be divided into two groups: the first group consists of Visegrad countries (i.e., Czechia, Slovakia, Hungary, and Poland) and Slovenia, and the second group includes countries from South and Eastern Europe (i.e., Romania, Bulgaria, Croatia, Serbia, and Bosnia and Herzegovina). The first group of Visegrad countries and Slovenia represents the EU member states with completed bank restructuring and privatization; countries with relatively high GDP per capita, small state share, and high share of foreign investors in the banking sector. Considering the stage of integration with the

EU, the level of economic development and development of the banking sector, the second group of countries is much more heterogeneous.

These countries have some common and different features. Their financial systems can be characterized as bank-oriented and concentrated on a model of universal banking. Banks have a dominant role in financial intermediation and thus play an important role in the economy of these countries. Except for Serbia and Bosnia and Herzegovina (that are candidates or potential candidates), all these countries joined the EU. Slovenia and Slovakia entered the Euro area. Financial groups are often present and systematically important in these countries. On the other side, the activities of banks in the financial markets significantly differ, as well as the macroeconomic conditions, the level of EU integration, and so forth. Therefore, an empirical analysis of banks from these banking sectors can yield interesting results.

To describe the selected banking sectors more briefly, it could be useful to provide some basic indicators. First, we will compare the countries' wealth and the importance of the banking sector in individual banking sectors. Then, we will focus on the number of banks operating in CEE banking sectors and their ownership.

Table 1 provides information about living standards in individual countries, that is, the GDP per capita, expressed in euro. Slovenia has the highest GDP per capita for the whole analysed period, accompanied or surpassed by Czechia during the second half of the period. The lowest values of this indicator were recorded in Bosnia and Herzegovina, Serbia, Bulgaria, and Romania. However, with some exceptions due to the global financial crisis, there is a significant upward trend in country's wealth in all CEE countries.

As the banking sectors in all CEE countries are bank-oriented, it is evident that relatively high degrees of financial intermediation are needed. Table 2 measures the degree of financial intermediation in individual countries as a share of total banking assets in GDP. Czechia and Croatia are countries with the highest degree of financial intermediation, Romania is on the opposite side of the rank with the lowest share of banking assets in GDP. There are several reasons why the level of banking financial intermediation is very low in Romania: on the demand side, credits are limited due to low enterprise density, poor health of enterprises, relatively high number of foreign-owned firms, and increasing use of other forms of financing; on the supply side, banks are adversely affected by high share of NPLs and deleveraging pressures (World Bank, 2018).

Total number of banks in individual banking sectors, including commercial banks, branches of foreign banks, building societies, and specialized banks is recorded in Table 3. The highest number of banks operates in the Polish banking sector, followed by Czechia. The least banks operate in

Table 1 GDP per capita in CEE countries (EUR thousands)

	05	06	07	08	09	10	11	12	13	14	15	16	17	18
BA	4.8	6.3	6.2	6.5	6.2	7.1	8.1	7.8	8.0	9.4	4.3	4.5	4.7	5.0
BG	4.2	4.5	4.8	5.1	4.9	5.1	5.3	5.4	5.4	5.5	5.7	5.9	6.1	6.3
CZ	13.7	14.5	15.3	15.5	14.7	15.0	15.3	15.2	15.2	15.5	16.3	16.7	17.5	18.0
HR	10.3	10.8	11.3	11.6	10.7	10.6	10.6	10.4	10.4	10.4	10.8	11.2	11.8	12.2
HU	9.9	10.4	10.4	10.5	9.9	10.0	10.2	10.1	10.3	10.8	11.2	11.5	12.0	12.7
PL	16.6	16.8	17.2	17.3	16.7	17.0	16.7	16.2	16.1	16.3	16.6	17.0	17.7	18.2
RO	5.1	5.6	6.1	6.7	6.4	6.2	6.4	6.5	6.8	7.0	7.3	7.7	8.3	8.7
RS	3.7	3.9	4.1	4.4	4.3	4.3	4.5	4.6	4.6	4.5	4.6	4.8	5.0	5.2
SK	10.0	10.8	11.9	12.6	11.9	12.6	13.0	13.2	13.3	13.6	14.3	14.6	15.0	15.5
SL	16.6	17.5	18.6	19.2	17.6	17.8	17.9	17.4	17.2	17.6	18.0	18.6	19.4	20.3

Source: Authors' processing based on data from Eurostat.

Table 2 Total banking assets in % of GDP

	05	06	07	08	09	10	11	12	13	14	15	16	17	18
BA	69.3	76.8	89.6	85.2	87.2	86.9	82.0	83.7	86.3	88.1	89.5	87.3	90.0	94.4
BG	76.8	85.5	98.2	100.4	104.6	104.6	97.9	103.0	106.8	103.6	101.3	98.3	97.2	98.2
CZ	97.7	97.4	108.4	107.5	113.0	114.7	114.7	118.2	127.6	126.4	124.0	126.2	140.1	138.4
HR	98.7	106.5	101.5	108.0	112.9	117.1	124.8	123.4	123.1	122.7	120.1	113.1	110.0	109.2
HU	90.1	99.1	106.8	118.6	134.0	123.1	123.7	109.8	103.4	99.5	96.9	99.3	96.8	95.3
PL	64.2	68.6	75.3	72.0	88.0	82.7	85.0	84.6	86.1	88.8	89.4	91.7	89.3	89.5
RO	45.1	50.9	62.5	66.0	72.7	73.7	69.5	67.9	64.1	60.6	58.7	56.1	53.6	51.0
RS	54.2	64.4	73.6	64.7	84.4	91.6	88.1	93.8	83.2	84.9	86.3	79.5	75.7	78.4
SK	98.7	88.4	68.8	97.4	84.1	82.9	79.5	80.5	80.9	83.4	86.5	88.1	89.2	88.7
SL	99.3	108.8	124.9	131.6	151.8	150.8	126.1	126.0	110.3	100.3	92.9	83.7	84.4	89.9

Source: Authors' processing based on data from CEE Banking Sector Reports published by Raiffeisen Bank International during the period 2005–20.

Table 3 Number of banks in CEE banking sectors

	05	06	07	08	09	10	11	12	13	14	15	16	17	18
Absolute number of banks														
BA	33	32	32	30	30	29	29	28	27	26	26	23	23	23
BG	34	32	29	30	30	30	31	31	30	28	28	27	27	25
CZ	36	37	37	37	39	41	44	43	44	45	46	45	47	50
HR	34	33	33	33	34	34	32	31	30	28	28	28	25	21
HU	33	29	38	38	35	35	35	35	35	35	35	37	36	35
PL	61	63	64	70	67	70	66	69	69	66	65	63	63	63
RO	39	38	41	42	41	41	40	39	39	39	35	36	34	33
RS	40	37	35	34	34	33	33	32	31	29	31	30	29	28
SK	23	24	25	26	26	29	31	28	28	28	27	27	26	27
SL	20	22	21	19	19	19	25	23	23	21	19	21	21	21
Number of inhabitants per bank (in thousands)														
BA	114	117	117	125	124	127	126	128	131	133	131	147	145	144
BG	225	237	260	249	248	246	237	235	242	258	256	263	262	281
CZ	283	276	278	280	267	255	238	244	238	233	229	234	225	212
HR	126	130	130	130	126	126	133	137	141	151	150	149	164	194
HU	305	347	264	264	286	285	284	283	282	282	281	265	271	279

Table 3 (cont.)

	05	06	07	08	09	10	11	12	13	14	15	16	17	18
PL	625	605	595	544	569	543	576	551	551	575	584	602	602	602
RO	546	557	509	489	496	493	503	514	512	510	566	547	576	590
RS	186	200	211	216	215	220	219	224	231	245	228	235	242	249
SK	233	223	214	206	207	185	174	193	193	193	200	201	209	201
SL	100	91	96	106	107	107	82	89	89	98	108	98	98	98

Source: Authors' processing and calculations based on data from the World Bank and CEE Banking Sector Reports published by Raiffeisen Bank International during the period 2005–20.

Slovenia, Croatia, or Slovakia. As we can see, the number of banks does not necessarily correspond to the share of banking assets in GDP.

To be able to assess the access to financial services, it could be useful to compare the number of banks to the number of inhabitants. Therefore, the second part of the Table 3 contains the number of inhabitants per one bank in each country. In spite of the highest absolute number of banks, we can see also the highest number of inhabitants and thus the lowest access to bank services in Poland. On the opposite side, the lowest number of operating banks but also the lowest number of inhabitants per bank and thus the highest access to the banking products and services were recorded for Slovenia. Even if the situation in other banking sectors is not so straightforward, we can conclude that the number of banks operating in particular banking sectors does not necessarily correspond either to the access to financial services or to the degree of financial intermediation.

It can be interesting also to see what is the ownership of banks, mainly what is the share of state ownership and foreign capital ownership. These indicators are recorded in Tables 4 and 5. Significantly, highest share of state in the banking sector can be found in Poland, followed by Serbia and Hungary.

At the same time, Poland and Hungary are the banking sectors with the lowest share of foreign capital, for Hungary, it is true mainly in the second half of the analysed period (Table 5). On the contrary, the majority of banks are owned by foreign owners in the case of Slovakia, Croatia, Czechia, and Bosnia and Herzegovina.

3.4 Selected Financial Conglomerates Operating in CEE Banking Sectors

With regard to financial conglomerates (or, to be more precise, as regards to financial groups), we consider the following institutions as appropriate: Erste Group, KBC Group, Raiffeisen Group, Société Générale Group, and UniCredit Group.

Erste Group was founded in 1819 as the first Austrian savings bank. Erste Group is one of the largest financial services providers in the eastern part of the EU in terms of clients and total assets. Banks belonging to the Erste Group are in top three banks in the core market in Czechia, Slovakia, Romania, and Hungary. Erste Group has an extensive presence in CEE market:

– Sparkasse Bank dd BiH (Bosnia and Herzegovina)
– Erste Bank Croatia and Erste & Steiermarkische Bank d.d. (Croatia)
– Česká spořitelna, a.s. (Czechia)
– Erste Bank Hungary Zrt. (Hungary)

Table 4 Market share of state-owned banks (% of total assets)

	05	06	07	08	09	10	11	12	13	14	15	16	17	18
BA	3.6	3.2	2	0.9	0.9	3.4	0.9	1	2	2.7	2.4	2.1	1.4	2.4
BG	0.3	0.3	2.1	2.1	2.4	3.2	3.7	3.3	3.4	3.7	3.2	3.5	4.1	4.4
CZ	3.6	3.3	2.5	2.8	2.7	3.3	3.2	2.8	2.4	2.3	2.2	1.8	1.2	1.1
HR	3.4	4.2	4.7	4.4	4.2	4.3	4.5	4.8	5.3	5.2	5.2	6.3	6.1	6.2
HU	n.a.	n.a.	n.a.	3.9	4.4	4.6	5.3	5.1	5.8	12.6	15.9	11.5	10.9	10.2
PL	21.3	19.6	18.3	17.3	20.8	21.5	22	21	20	18	18	32	34	32.5
RO	6	5.5	5.4	5.2	7.3	7.4	8.2	8.4	8.5	8.8	8.3	8.2	8.7	8.1
RS	24.1	15.3	16.5	17.5	18.2	20.3	19.7	19	18.5	19.2	17.9	18.1	16.4	16.4
SK	1.8	1.1	1	0.8	0.9	5.3	0.9	0.8	0.8	0.9	0.8	0.8	0.7	0.7
SL	18.1	17.9	15.1	17.7	20.5	20.1	47	45	61	60	61	48	n.a.	n.a.

Source: Authors' processing based on data from CEE Banking Sector Reports published by Raiffeisen Bank International during the period 2005–20.

Table 5 Market share of foreign-owned banks (% of total assets)

	05	06	07	08	09	10	11	12	13	14	15	16	17	18
BA	91	94	94	95	95	97	92	92	90	84	85	86	86	85
BG	80	80	82	84	83	81	75	74	70	76	76	76	77	76
CZ	94	97	96	88	87	87	84	82	83	85	84	85	87	86
HR	91	91	90	91	91	90	91	90	90	90	89	90	90	90
HU	84	82	78	91	91	90	89	89	89	64	44	45	45	41
PL	70	66	67	67	63	66	66	63	62	60	61	55	54	54
RO	62	89	88	88	85	85	83	90	90	90	90	91	77	75
RS	69	79	76	75	74	73	73	69	75	75	76	76	76	77
SK	97	99	97	96	94	93	989	98.6	99	99	99	99	99	99
SL	39	40	38	38	36	37	29	31	33	35	33	46	n.a.	n.a.

Source: Authors' processing based on data from CEE Banking Sector Reports published by Raiffeisen Bank International during the period 2005–20.

- Banca Comerciala Romana SA (Romania)
- Slovenska sporitelna, a.s. (Slovakia)
- Erste Bank a.d. Novi Sad (Serbia).

KBC, a Belgian group, was formed in 1998 after the merger of two Belgian banks and a Belgian insurance company. Belgium, Czechia, Slovakia, Hungary, Bulgaria, and Ireland are the core markets. In CEE countries, KBC Group operates with the following brands:

- United Bulgarian Bank AD (Bulgaria)
- Československá obchodní banka, a.s. (Czechia)
- K&H Bank Zrt. (Hungary)
- Československá obchodná banka, a.s. (Slovakia).

Raiffeisen Group is an Austrian banking group. Raiffeisen Group has more than thirty years of experience in the region of CEE countries, as its first subsidiary bank was founded in Hungary in 1986. As Raiffeisen Group regards CEE countries as its home market, Raiffeisen Group operates in most CEE countries (compared with other analysed financial groups):

- Raiffeisen Bank dd. Bosna I Hercegovina (Bosnia and Herzegovina)
- Raiffeisenbank (Bulgaria) EAD (Bulgaria)
- Raiffeisenbank Austria d.d. (Croatia)
- Raiffeisenbank a.s. (Czechia)
- Raiffeisen Bank Zrt. (Hungary)
- Raiffeisen Bank SA (Romania)
- Raiffeisenbank a.d. (Serbia)
- Tatra banka, a.s. (Slovakia).

Société Générale is a French banking and financial services company head-quartered in Paris. Société Générale was founded in 1864 in France. In 1998, Société Générale set up retail banking outside France (in Romania and Bulgaria). Société Générale Group operates in the following CEE countries:

- Société Générale Expresbank (Bulgaria)
- Komerční Banka (Czechia)
- Euro Bank SA (Poland) – till 2019
- BRD – Groupe Société Générale (Romania)
- Société Générale Banka Srbija (Serbia)
- SKB Banka (Slovenia).

UniCredit is an Italian banking and financial company. UniCredit Group was the outcome of the merger of several Italian banks in 1998. In 1999, UniCredito

Italiano began its expansion in Eastern Europe (with the acquisition of Polish Bank Pekao). UniCredit Group CEE network includes the following countries:

- UniCredit Bank d.d. and UniCredit Bank Banja Luka (Bosnia and Herzegovina)
- UniCredit Bulbank (Bulgaria)
- Zagrebačka banka d.d. (Croatia)
- UniCredit Bank Czech Republic and Slovakia (Czechia)
- UniCredit Bank Hungary Zrt. (Hungary)
- UniCredit Bank Romania (Romania)
- UniCredit Bank Serbia (Serbia)
- UniCredit Bank Slovenia (Slovenia).

Market shares of each financial group in analysed countries are presented in Table 6. As we can see, Czech, Romanian, and Slovak banking sectors are the most important for Erste Group. KBC Group reaches highest market share in Slovenian and Czech banking sectors. For Raiffeisen Group, Bosnia and Herzegovina, Croatia, and Slovakia are the most important countries. Societe Generale has the highest market share in Czech and Romanian banking sector, UniCredit Group in Croatian, Bulgarian and Bosnian banking sector.

4 Methodology and Data

The first part of this section explains the construction of an aggregate index of financial stability. The second part of the section describes the data used for the empirical analysis.

4.1 The Aggregate Index of Financial Stability

Financial stability may also be measured by the aggregate index. As some ratios are typically good, while some other ratios are bad, it may be difficult to assess the overall financial health of the analysed institution/system. This is the reason why aggregate index construction may be a useful policy tool for identifying trends, drawing attention to various phenomena, benchmarking country performance, interpreting results, and communicating the findings to the public (Karanovic and Karanovic, 2015).

An aggregate financial stability index has many advantages: (i) it can summarize complex, multidimensional realities with a view to support decision-makers; (ii) it is easier to interpret; (iii) it can assess progress over time; (iv) it reduces the visible size of a set of indicators, without dropping the underlying information base, and thus make it possible to include more information; and

Table 6 Market share of selected financial groups in selected CEE countries (% of total assets)

	Erste		KBC		Raiffeisen		Soc. Generale		UniCredit	
	05	18	05	18	05	18	05	18	05	18
BA	1.33	4.55	-	-	21.20	14.21	-	-	16.02	24.61
BG	-	-	9.69	10.67	8.55	7.37	-	-	10.38	18.39
CZ	18.41	19.45	21.83	18.79	2.60	4.94	16.90	14.45	5.67	9.00
HR	11.66	14.76	-	-	10.86	7.84	-	-	24.36	27.21
HU	7.36	6.12	9.84	8.04	6.35	6.02	-	-	0.54	7.60
PL	-	-	-	-	-	-	0.32	0.76	-	-
RO	25.35	13.97	-	-	8.57	8.24	14.80	11.12	6.97	8.54
RS	1.32	4.66	-	-	13.18	7.34	3.69	7.95	8.42	11.00
SK	22.19	21.73	15.90	10.63	15.79	16.18	-	-	-	-
SL	-	-	32.60	20.45	-	-	6.80	7.38	6.63	6.42

Source: Authors' calculation.

(v) it enables users to compare complex dimensions effectively. Disadvantages of the index are connected mainly with its poor construction or misinterpretation: (i) it may send misleading policy messages and may invite simplistic policy conclusions; (ii) it may lead to inappropriate policies; and (iii) it may disguise serious failings in some dimensions and increase the difficulty of identifying proper remedial action (OECD, 2008).

The construction of an aggregate financial stability index can be found in the works of quite many authors. Most studies focus on application of the created aggregate financial stability index on just one single country, such as Czechia (Geršl and Heřmánek, 2008), Slovakia (Laznia, 2013), Romania (Albulescu, 2010; Roman and Sargu, 2013), Albania (BOA, 2010), Macedonia (Petrovska and Mihajlovska, 2013), Lithuania (Ginevičius and Podviezko, 2013), Latvia (Kondratovs, 2014), Netherlands (Van den End and Tabbae, 2005; Van den End, 2006), Switzerland (SNB, 2006), Spain (Maudos, 2012), Turkey (CBRT, 2006; Altan et al., 2014), Canada (Illing and Liu, 2003), United States (Nelson and Perli, 2007), or India (Mishra et al., 2013). Only a few studies concern more countries, such as the Euro Area countries (Albulescu, 2013), Balkan countries (Karanovic and Karanovic, 2015), or countries that joined EU in 2004 (Kočišová and Stavárek, 2018).

Geršl and Heřmánek (2008) describe five approaches for the construction of the aggregate financial stability index: (i) A relatively simple aggregate index can be constructed as a weighted average of partial indicators of the financial soundness of banks, such as in CBRT (2006). (ii) An alternative method is to construct an index using daily data from the financial markets which enables one to signal any difficulties in the financial sector in advance, such as in Nelson and Perli (2007) or Illing and Liu (2003). (iii) A sensible approach combines information from the financial markets with information from the financial statements of financial institutions, as in SNB (2006). (iv) An original approach was used in the Netherlands – the index is constructed on the basis of an enlarged monetary conditions index; they introduced upper and lower critical limits to consider potential non-linear effects (Van den End, 2006). (v) It is also possible to calculate the default risk at the level of the entire financial system using the Merton model (Van den End and Tabbae, 2005; Čihák, 2007). Obviously, individual studies differ not only by methodology but also by the variables included in the aggregate index. Kočišová et al. (2018) provided a detailed literature review and an overview of the indicators used in these studies. According to Geršl and Heřmánek (2008), most of the attempts to construct an aggregate financial stability index focus on the banking sector, which is the most important part of the financial system with respect to financial stability. As a result, aggregate index typically consists of some ratios on bank profitability, liquidity, asset quality, and solvency. Exchange rate risk and interest rate risk ratios are also important, at least in some studies. Some authors also take into consideration the impact of macroeconomic and market conditions, such as the development of rate of inflation, share of budget deficit, and/or current account deficit on gross domestic product, concentration ratios, or asset prices. However, we can summarize that in most studies dealing with bank stability assessment, attention is concentrated on four main areas: capital adequacy, quality of assets, profitability, and liquidity. These areas are in line with the so-called CAMELS methodology which is normally used for the assessment of financial institutions' soundness.

The aggregate index of the financial stability, used in this Element for empirical analysis, will be based on indicators of performance, liquidity, solvency, and asset quality. Therefore, the proposed indicator is based on the banking sector data.

We consider banking performance as one part of the stability of banks. In general, banking performance is defined as the achievement of the objectives set forth by the bank within the agreed time and with minimal costs while using the available resources. Performance is indicated by banking efficiency and profitability. The reasons for considering banking efficiency in the stability index are several. First, the banking efficiency provides one value about banking performance; moreover, it is comparable within other banks. Shaddady and Moore (2019) added Data Envelopment Analysis (DEA) to the financial stability investigation model and used CAMELS–DEA. Moreover, in the empirical literature, several authors showed the relationship between efficiency and banking stability. For example, Kwan and Eisenbeis (1997) and Fiordelisi et al. (2011) found that inefficient banks seem to take less risk; therefore, inefficiency has a positive impact on risk-taking. Kaffash et al. (2018) found that the banking Z-score was negatively associated with the technical efficiency. Their finding shows that banks operating in a market with the relatively lower risk of a banking crisis are more efficient. Therefore, the other reason for using efficiency into the financial stability index is the existence of the relationship between efficiency and banking risks that can influence banking stability. As Fiordelisi et al. (2011) concluded, improvements in bank efficiency cause a lower probability of default.

We measure banking efficiency using non-parametric method, namely: dynamic DEA. Bogetoft and Otto (2011) summarized that the non-parametric models are the most flexible in terms of the production economic properties that can be invoked. We measure the technical efficiency of banks using an input-oriented model with variable return to scale. We use the dynamic DEA model; it is an actual methodology that assesses the relative efficiency of banks. Although the dynamic DEA requires the strictly balanced panel data, we are not able to consider newly established banks and banks that merge during the period 2005–18. Theoretical description of the DEA model presents Palečková (2018). In order to conduct the DEA estimation, inputs and outputs need to be defined. In line with the intermediation approach, we use three inputs (labour, physical capital, and total deposits) and two outputs (total loans and other earning assets).

Profitability indicators measure the ability to absorb losses without any impact on capital and to realize business goals and plans (Pavković et al., 2018). The methodology on profitability indicators is described in Palečková (2018). The traditional profitability indicators are ROA, return on equity, net interest margin (NIM), cost to income ratio, and net non-interest margin. We use the ROA and the NIM. ROA is an important measure of the bank's stability. If banking stability is measured using the Z-score, the ROA is the key indicator. Although in the empirical literature there is mixed evidence, the authors suggested the impact of bank profitability on banking stability (e.g., Berger et al., 2009; Natalya et al., 2015). The ROA and NIM in the financial stability index are commonly used in previous studies (see e.g., Kočišová and Stavárek, 2018) as well as in the financial stability index measured by the CNB.

Liquidity means the resilience of the bank to cash flow shocks. This ability to withstand shocks enhances financial stability. To assess bank liquidity, for example, the following liquidity ratios are commonly employed: the liquid asset ratio (LIA), the loan-to-asset ratio, the loan-to-deposit (LTD) ratio, and the net interbank position (Vodová, 2013). We will include two ratios into the aggregate index of financial stability: the LIA and the LTD ratio. The LIA is the most widely used measure of bank liquidity. It belongs to the core IMF Soundness indicators. Also, Geršl and Heřmánek (2008), Karanovic and Karanovic (2015), Akosah et al. (2018), and Kočišová and Stavárek (2018) used this ratio. Geršl and Heřmánek (2008) also used the share of liquid assets in clients' deposits. Kočišová and Stavárek (2018) calculated, in accordance with the core IMF Soundness indicators, the share of liquid assets in short-term liabilities. However, these two ratios focus on the same aspect of bank liquidity (liquid asset buffer) but are only related to liabilities. We choose an innovative approach: to assess also the vulnerability of bank to development on the interbank market, we will use as a second ratio, the LTD ratio. If the value of this ratio is higher than 100 per cent, banks need also other sources for financing its lending activity (clients' deposits are not sufficient), which makes it much more vulnerable, especially during market turmoil.

Financial stability is also positively influenced also by bank solvency. Solvency ratios measure the bank's ability to absorb sudden losses and are thus closest to the resilience to shocks. There exist many indicators of solvency; some of them are determined by legislation. We will use the capital ratio or level of capitalization (CAP), which measures the share of equity in total assets. Our approach is in accordance with Altan et al. (2014), Roman and Sargu (2013), and Karanovic and Karanovic (2015).

We could also use some of the core IMF Soundness indicators: regulatory capital to risk-weighted assets, regulatory tier 1 capital to risk-weighted assets, and NPLs net provisions to capital. However, we prefer CAP as this ratio is directly related to default risk because a higher capital ratio suggests that the bank has more equity capital to cover its debt liability and loan losses, and therefore it is less likely to default.

Financial stability may be jeopardized by excessive credit risk. To measure the asset quality ratio, we will follow Geršl and Heřmánek (2008), Kočišová and Stavárek (2018), and Karanovic and Karanovic (2015) and focus on the share of NPLs in total gross loans. The core IMF Soundness indicators contain also the sectoral distribution of loans to total loans. This ratio cannot be used due to data availability. The disadvantage of another possible indicator, the share of loan loss provisions in total gross loans, lies in the fact that its values are strongly influenced by different bank's policies for loan collateral and provisioning.

As mentioned earlier in this section, most of the disadvantages of the aggregate index arise from its poor construction. To avoid such problems, we will follow the methodology recommended by OECD (2008), which divided the construction of an aggregate index into the following steps: (i) theoretical framework, (ii) data selection, (iii) imputation of missing data, (iv) multivariate analysis, (v) normalization, (vi) weighting and aggregation, (vii) robustness and sensitivity, (viii) back to the real data and links to other variables.

A theoretical framework must be developed to provide the basis for the selection and combination of single ratios into a meaningful aggregate index. Our aim is to construct an aggregate financial stability index which will assess the financial stability of banks from CEE countries.

When selecting data, ratios should be chosen on the basis of their analytical soundness, measurability, country coverage, relevance to the phenomenon being measured, and relationship to each other. Our aggregate index includes three indicators of performance (the ROA and NIM as indices of profitability and banking efficiency using DEA), two ratios of liquidity (the LIA and the share of net interbank position in total assets), one ratio of solvency (the total capital ratio), and one ratio of credit risk, that is, asset quality (the share of NPLs in total loans). For banks that belong to a financial conglomerate, we will add the stability of the parent company. We suppose that financial problems of the parent company can influence its subsidiaries. We did not have to deal with missing data, as data availability was one of the important factors in choosing individual financial ratios and individual banks.

First, the indicators which in opposite directions show improvement/deterioration in terms of the direction of other indicators, their reciprocal value is taken. Therefore, in this study, the indicator of the quality of assets is multiplied by (−1).

In order to aggregate the variables into a single index, each indicator is normalized to allow for comparability between variables. Several methods of normalization are discussed in the literature along with their shortcomings (Morris, 2011). We used the method of empirical normalization. The indicators are normalized through a process of empirical normalization that placed all indicators in the interval from 0 to 1. Whereas a value of zero shows the worst value of an indicator, the value of 1 represents the best value of this indicator. The formula of empirical normalization is (Cheang and Choy, 2009):

$$I_{it}^n = \frac{I_{it} - \text{Min}(I_i)}{\text{Max}(I_i) - \text{Min}(I_i)}, \tag{1}$$

where I_{it}^n represents the normalized indicator at time t, I_{it} is the value of indicator i in period t; $\text{Min}(I_i)$ and $\text{Max}(I_i)$ are the minimum and maximum of the indicator in the analysed period.

The ratios should be weighted and aggregated according to the underlying theoretical framework. The process of weighting will be described precisely later in this section.

Sensitivity analysis can help gauge the robustness of the aggregate index and improve transparency. It assesses the contribution of the individual source of uncertainty to the variance in output. The analysis of sensitivity with the use of scenario analysis will be the content of our future research.

Back to the real data and links to other variables. The aggregate index should be transparent and fit to be decomposed into its underlying ratios. This will enable us to investigate the contribution of individual areas of banking business to overall financial stability of banks, especially the link between financial stability of the parent company and its subsidiary bank.

For the aggregate financial stability index for all banks in the sample, we will follow the methodology of Kočišová and Stavárek (2018). The aggregate index is constructed as a weighted sum of selected indicators. As already mentioned, we will consider three indicators of performance, two ratios of liquidity, one ratio of solvency, one ratio of credit risk, and the financial stability of the parent company, where applicable. The main categories of the index, their weights, selected ratios, and their expected impact on the financial stability index are presented in Table 7.

Table 7 Aggregate financial stability index for individual
banks

Category	Weight	Ratios	Impact
Performance	0.25	DEA	+
		ROA	+
		NIM	+
Liquidity	0.25	LAR	+
		LTD	−
Solvency	0.25	CAP	+
Asset quality	0.25	NPL	−

Source: Authors' processing.

Before the final aggregation, the data will pass through a process of normalization and weights' allocation, in order to place the values of the ratios on the same scale and to ensure that the development of the ratios had the same effects on the development of the index. First, in the case of the ratio with negative impact on financial stability (NPL and LTD), we will take the reciprocal value of it to ensure that the increase of this ratio will mean the increase in financial stability. Second, we have to normalize the ratios. We will use empirical normalization which means that all ratios will be placed on the same scale in the interval from zero to one. Third, the average values of the first and second categories (e.g., for performance and liquidity) will be calculated using the variance equal weights method, which is the most common weighting method used in the literature (Kočišová and Stavárek, 2018). To put it simply, we use the same weight for each indicator to calculate the sub-indicator of the aggregate financial stability index, for example, in case of performance we consider bank efficiency (measured using DEA), ROA, and NIM to calculate the sub-indicator that measures the bank performance. Finally, the aggregate financial stability index is calculated for all banks in the sample in each year as a sum of weighted values for four individual components. In the other words, the normalized sub-indicators are then combined into a single index. We assign the same weight to all individual indicators in order to calculate the composite indices in case we do not consider the parent company. We consider the equivalent contribution of each of sub-indices in the overall assessment of the bank. Moreover, the similar approach is used in CAMEL. The same weight to indicators was used in studies of, for example, Kočišová and Stavárek (2018) and Alakbarov et al. (2018).

We can expect some differences between small and large banks. According to empirical studies, large banks have lower NIM than small banks (Horváth, 2009), large banks are less efficient (Inanoglu et al., 2016), larger banks usually rely more on funds from the interbank market (Berrospide, 2013; Cornett et al., 2012), banks that are net lenders on the interbank market tend to be smaller than borrower banks (Lucchetta, 2007), large banks have smaller capital buffer than small banks (Jokipii and Milne, 2008; Stolz and Wedow, 2011; Klepková Vodová, 2019), and quality of the loan portfolio of large banks is better (Salas and Saurina, 2002; Curak et al., 2013). It is logical that differences in the values of individual ratios will influence the value of the aggregate index.

In case of banks that belong to a financial conglomerate, the aggregate financial stability index will also include the indicator of the financial stability of their parent company (aggregate financial stability index of a parent company). This indicator will be calculated as an aggregate financial stability index (i.e., according to the methodology described in Table 7). The main categories of the index for banks belonging to a financial conglomerate, their weights, selected ratios, and their expected impact on the whole financial stability index are presented in Table 8. We assign the same weight to bank indicators (performance, liquidity, solvency, and asset quality), and the parent company's financial stability has an assigned weight of 10 per cent. Most of the banks in CEE have become part of a financial group during the consolidation and privatization in the banking sector. The transition process from plan to market has proven to be an opportunity for many foreign banks to expand their activities to CEE, either through establishing greenfields or through taking over former state-owned banks (De Haas and Van Lelyveld, 2006). However, in CEE, banks operate as separate units, and they adapt their operations to the

Table 8 Aggregate financial stability index for banks that belong to a financial conglomerate

Category	Weight	Ratios	Impact
Performance	0.225	DEA	+
		ROA	+
		NIM	+
Liquidity	0.225	LAR	+
		LTD	+
Solvency	0.225	CAP	+
Asset quality	0.225	NPL	−
Affiliation with the fin. conglomerate	0.100	Aggregate index of a parent company	+

Source: Authors' processing.

local banking market, the responsibility lies with the local bank management. In other words, in CEE, the foreign bank subsidiaries react not so much to changes in the parent bank's home country but rather to changes in local economic conditions (see De Haas and Van Lelyveld, 2006). Therefore, we assume lower impact of the parent company on subsidiaries. Higher weight is assigned to the bank-specific indicators. Moreover, Pietrzak (2021) claimed that the indicators that should be closely monitored to accurate and early detection of distress are related to the capital adequacy and profitability of deposit taker institutions.

All possible values of the aggregate financial stability index can be placed in the interval from zero to one. Obviously, higher values of the aggregate index indicate higher financial stability of the bank. However, to be able to interpret differences in financial stability of individual banks more properly, it could be useful to divide the possible values of the index into several bands. Therefore, we will apply the following threshold values for both types of indices (see Table 9).

Excellent values of the aggregate index of financial stability can be reached only by banks with excellent performance (both in terms of profitability and efficiency), outstanding liquidity and solvency, and superior credit portfolio, and whose parent company is financially stable, too. With a decrease in the value of the index, financial stability decreases. Banks with poor financial stability are banks that are loss making, inefficient, illiquid, insolvent, their credit portfolio includes high share of NPLs, and their parent company is not financial stable either. We will indicate each band with a special colour. This will enable us to present our results more clearly.

4.2 Data Used

The research will focus on the region of CEE. We will particularly consider Czechia, Slovakia, Hungary, Poland, Romania, Bulgaria, Croatia, Serbia,

Table 9 Threshold values for the aggregate financial stability index

Value of the agg. index	Colour marking	Fin. stability of a bank/ parent company
0.00–0.29		Poor
0.30–0.39		Below standard
0.40–0.49		Average
0.50–0.69		Very good
0.70–1.00		Excellent

Source: Authors' processing.

Bosnia and Herzegovina, and Slovenia. Regarding financial groups, among others; we consider the following institutions as appropriate: Erste Group, KBC Group, Raiffeisen Group, Société Générale Group, and UniCredit Group. As data sources, we will use mainly the databases Orbis BankFocus and data obtained from annual reports of commercial banks and financial groups. The data set covers the period 2005–18.

Our initial sample includes 138 banks from 10 CEE countries where the banks belonging to the financial conglomerates operate. Data from individual banks are unconsolidated. To avoid unreliable data, only banks that were present on the market for the entire period were chosen in our sample. From our point of view, small and new developed banks will not affect financial stability as much as large banks and banks have been on the market for a longer period. Moreover, we applied the dynamic DEA approach to assess the efficiency of the banking sector, and this approach requires the strictly balanced panel data. Therefore, the data set included a sample of 1932 observation. The coverage of banking sector assets in our data set amounts to around 75 per cent of the banking sector assets in average country (see Table 10). Our sample includes also small banks. The reason of inclusion of also small banks is twofold: (i) it enables us to cover significant part of all particular banking sectors; and (ii) we are able to compare results of aggregate index of financial stability for small, medium sized, and large banks, and for banks that belong and do not belong to any financial group (so we can see the effects of the affiliation). Moreover, the data set includes five financial conglomerates (five parent companies) where the consolidated data are considered.

For the estimation of technical efficiency, it is necessary to define the inputs and outputs. Consistently with the intermediation approach, we assume that banks use the three inputs: labour measured by the total number of employees, physical capital measured by fixed assets and total deposits, and two outputs: total loans and other earning assets. Palečková (2018) provides detailed information on the construction of the dynamic DEA model and the selection of inputs and outputs. The descriptive statistics of the data sets used for individual commercial banks in ten CEE countries are presented in Table 11, and the descriptive statistics for five financial conglomerates are presented in Table 12.

5 Empirical Analysis

To fulfil the threefold aim of this Element, the structure of this section is as follows. The first part of the section presents the results for all CEE banks included in the sample and for their parent companies (see Appendix 1 for the explanation of the abbreviation used). We also present the financial

Table 10 Market share of analysed banks (in %)

	2005	2006	2007	2008	2009	2010	2011	2012	2013	2014	2015	2016	2017	2018
BA	72	71	72	78	79	77	77	77	77	78	82	83	82	82
BG	72	75	84	84	83	81	80	77	77	85	92	90	89	92
CZ	73	73	71	70	72	72	74	75	77	76	79	81	81	82
HR	77	79	77	80	77	78	77	79	80	81	82	84	84	92
HU	60	61	63	64	64	66	67	67	63	64	64	62	60	60
PL	51	50	55	54	52	57	58	59	61	63	65	62	60	59
RO	61	64	59	54	51	51	53	52	52	53	58	59	60	62
RS	71	76	76	78	77	76	77	80	81	82	82	83	88	89
SK	82	78	79	74	78	77	77	75	76	75	76	77	80	81
SL	85	82	78	77	76	72	81	77	76	83	87	86	85	85

Source: Authors' calculation.

Table 11 Descriptive statistics of individual banks (in mil EUR)

	Mean	Median	Min	Max	St. Dev.
Total assets	4,669,803	1,695,558	9,200	69,784,636	7,972,009
Total equity	512,809	184,614	−797	8,910,861	891,405
Total deposits	3,218,284	1,007,041	1	57,475,057	5,765,073
Total loans	2,734,933	1,004,802	10	44,547,447	4,759,311
Liquid assets	863,199	262,909	101	20,035,501	1,629,706
Fixed assets	284,505	17,818	1	455,771,963	10,368,417
Number or employees	2688	883	14	80,795	7,045
Other earning assets	1,406,897	325,889	8	28,165,818	2,925,481
Profit before tax	46,592	9214	−1,466,800	1,111,358	143,614
NPL	295,270	120,347	0	4,948,995	501,456

Source: Authors' calculation.

Table 12 Descriptive statistics of selected financial conglomerates (in bil EUR)

	Mean	Median	Min	Max	St. Dev.
Total assets	531,193	271,155	40,695	1,382,241	432,875
Total equity	27,815	16,975	3,277	65,809	19,701
Total deposits	211,585	179,364	24,890	478,988	130,910
Total loans	243,511	147,855	24,714	613,872	173,707
Liquid assets	100,592	55,650	6,420	492,004	117,976
Fixed assets	6,588	2,394	739	26,751	6,442
Number or employees	84,523	55,630	26,941	174,519	49,787
Other earning assets	330,099	183,241	3,783	1,085,449	382,489
Profit before tax	204,999	154,145	−250,800	1,106,100	206,886
NPL	11,133	9,962	3,193	28,350	6,587

Source: Authors' calculation.

stability of selected financial conglomerates. The second part of the section focuses on the financial stability of banks that belong to a financial conglomerate, namely: on the effect of the affiliation with the financial conglomerate on the financial stability of individual banks and corresponding banking sectors. In order to achieve the highest possible clarity of the tables presented in this section, we have divided the total analysed period into three time periods: from 2005 to 2007 (which means the pre-crisis period), from 2008 to 2012 (which covers the period of double crisis), and the period from 2013 to 2018 (post-crisis period). We present the average values of the given variable for each time period in all tables. The detailed results (for individual years) are available in Appendixes 2–5.

5.1 Aggregate Financial Stability Index for Individual Banks from CEE Countries and Selected Financial Conglomerates

First of all, we will have a look on the financial stability of selected financial conglomerates (Table 13). The values of the aggregate indices are essential, as they act as an input for the calculation of the aggregate index of banks belonging to this financial group.

We can see significant differences among the selected financial groups. Erste Group and Raiffeisen Group reached the highest financial stability during the whole analysed period. Their financial stability can be marked as very good (it means that values of the index range between 0.5 and 0.69; it is indicated by yellow colour)

Table 13 Aggregate financial stability index for financial conglomerates
(parent companies)

Groups	2005–2007	2008–2012	2013–2018
Erste Group	0.58	0.61	0.68
Societe Generale	0.50	0.47	0.50
KBC Group	0.63	0.58	0.62
UniCredit Group	0.49	0.51	0.56
Raiffeisen Group	0.60	0.66	0.68

Source: Authors' calculations.

or even excellent (green; values of the index range between 0.7 and 1.0) – see Appendix 2. In the case of both financial conglomerates, it is caused mainly by excellent profitability (both in terms of ROA and NIM), sufficient solvency and liquidity, and favourable asset quality. On the contrary, Societe Generale Group is less financially stable, the values of its index indicate only average financial stability in most years (orange colour is a sign that the index ranges between 0.4 and 0.49). Although the majority of areas of financial stability are without any serious problem, Societe Generale Group has very low efficiency.

Now we will focus on individual countries. As it can be seen from Appendix 2, the financial stability of most banks in Bosnia and Herzegovina is average. Only Bosnia Bank, Investiciono-Komercijalna Banka, and Komercijalno-Investiciona Banka (all banks mainly due to excellent performance, relatively good solvency, and liquidity) have very good financial stability for the whole analysed period. Only one bank in one year had financial stability below standard (it is marked with red colour; values of the index range between 0.3 and 0.39 in that case); the efficiency of this bank is generally very low, the asset quality was very unfavourable, and moreover, this bank had liquidity problems (very low share of liquid assets) in 2008. On 14 December 2009, the Republic of Austria purchased 100 per cent of the shares in the Hypo Alpe-Adria_Bank International, the parent company of the Hypo Alpe-Adria-Bank.

There is no development trend common to all banks; there are some banks whose stability declined between 2005 and 2018, some banks whose stability increased, and some banks whose stability remained approximately the same. Four banks (Sparkasse Bank, Raiffeisenbank, UniCredit Bank Banja Luka, and UniCredit Bank) belong to three financial conglomerates (Erste Group, Raiffeisen Group, and UniCredit Group), so we considered financial stability of the parent company while calculating the financial stability index of these banks.

Table 14 Average values of aggregate financial stability index for Bosnian banks belonging to a financial group

Banks	2005–2007	2008–2012	2013–2018
Banking sector	0.49	0.48	0.47
Sparkasse	0.49	0.46	0.44
Erste Group	0.58	0.61	0.68
Raiffeisen	0.45	0.45	0.47
Raiffeisen Group	0.60	0.66	0.68
UniCredit BL	0.44	0.44	0.45
UniCredit	0.51	0.52	0.46
UniCredit Group	0.49	0.51	0.56

Source: Authors' calculations.

Table 15 Average values of aggregate financial stability index for Bulgarian banks belonging to a financial group

Banks	2005–2007	2008–2012	2013–2018
Banking sector	0.48	0.46	0.47
United Bulg.	0.43	0.41	0.45
KBC Group	0.63	0.58	0.62
Raiffeisen	0.51	0.52	0.42
Raiffeisen Group	0.60	0.66	0.68
UniCredit	0.47	0.46	0.47
UniCredit Group	0.49	0.51	0.56

Source: Authors' calculations.

As is visible from Table 14, all parent companies reached higher levels of financial stability than average banks from Bosnia and Herzegovina. However, this fact did not manifest in values of aggregate index of individual banks, which is usually even below average values for the whole banking sector (with the only exception of UniCredit Bank).

In the case of Bulgaria (Appendix 2, Table 15), we can see a slightly lower level of bank stability, when compared to Bosnia and Herzegovina. Again, the majority of banks recorded average financial stability (indicated by orange colour). Only the financial stability of Raiffeisenbank was very good for the whole period (mainly due to very good profitability and efficiency). First Investment Bank is on the opposite: its financial stability was below standard during 2009–13 (due to extremely low efficiency and low buffer of liquid assets).

Table 16 Average values of aggregate financial stability index for Czech banks belonging to a financial group

Banks	2005–2007	2008–2012	2013–2018
Banking sector	0.49	0.48	0.48
Sporitelna	0.49	0.50	0.50
Erste Group	0.58	0.61	0.68
CSOB	0.51	0.49	0.50
KBC Group	0.63	0.58	0.62
Komercni	0.51	0.49	0.48
Soc. Generale Group	0.50	0.47	0.50
Raiffeisen	0.49	0.49	0.50
Raiffeisen Group	0.60	0.66	0.68
UniCredit	0.48	0.48	0.49
UniCredit Group	0.49	0.51	0.56

Source: Authors' calculations.

Three banks (Raiffeisenbank, UniCredit Bulbank, and United Bulgarian Bank) belonged during the analysed period to three financial conglomerates (Raiffeisen Group, UniCredit Group, and KBC Group). The results again do not show any development trend common for most banks.

Results for Czech banks are presented in Table 16 and Appendix 2. In the beginning of our analysed period, the index has been fluctuating in yellow colour in case of eight banks. It supported the results of Geršl and Heřmánek (2008), who stated that the reason for the improving stability was the favourable phase of the business cycle, associated with economic growth and low interest rates. As the majority of orange colour indicates, most banks in most years reached only average level of financial stability. There are some exceptions. In most years, the financial stability of PPF banka is very good, mainly due to perfect performance and good liquidity. Equa banka has good level profitability and efficiency and held lots of liquid assets in the first half of the analysed period, which had a positive effect on its financial stability. On the other hand, Wüstenrot hypoteční banka recorded the lowest value of the stability index, mainly due to low liquidity and solvency (however, a lower level of liquidity is a result of the specialization of the bank: deposits are not a major source of financing of loan activity for mortgage banks, so the need for a buffer of liquid assets is naturally lower). Five banks (Česká spořitelna, ČSOB, Komerční banka, Raiffeisenbank, and UniCredit Bank) belong to financial conglomerates. Financial stability of Česká spořitelna and ČSOB is the highest and above

Table 17 Average values of aggregate financial stability index for Croatian
banks belonging to a financial group

Banks	2005–2007	2008–2012	2013–2018
Banking sector	0.49	0.49	0.50
Erste	0.47	0.47	0.48
Erste Group	0.58	0.61	0.68
Raiffeisen	0.47	0.48	0.49
Raiffeisen Group	0.60	0.66	0.68
Zagrebacka	0.49	0.48	0.47
UniCredit Group	0.49	0.51	0.56

Source: Authors' calculations

average for the Czech banking sector. Raiffeisenbank and UniCredit bank
reached lower level of financial stability than their parent companies; on the
contrary, financial stability of Komercni banka is higher than financial
stability of Societe Generale, at least till 2012.

In regard to Croatian banks, the orange colour (and thus average financial
stability) prevails (Table 17, Appendix 2). Looking at individual banks, the
highest values of the stability index were reached by BKS Bank and Privredna
Banka (due to good performance and solvency) and the lowest value by OTP
banka (it has low efficiency and liquidity). Erste & Steiermärkische Bank,
Raiffeisenbank, and Zagrebacka Banka belong to three financial conglomerates
(Erste Group, Raiffeisen Group, and UniCredit Group). Among them,
Zagrebacka Banka is the most financially stable. However, as in case of banks
from Bosnia and Herzegovina, financial stability of Croatian banks belonging to
any of analysed financial group is even below average of the whole banking
sector.

In the case of Hungarian banks (Table 18, Appendix 2), we cannot see any
extreme values, too. Budapest Bank and Sberbank are the representatives of
more fragile banks: the first one due to low efficiency, and the second one due to
insufficient solvency. OTP banka followed by UniCredit Bank are the banks that
are the most financially stable; both of them due to good performance and
sufficient liquidity. During the last years of the analysed period, also financial
stability of Erste Bank, Raiffeisen Bank, and K&H Bank is very good (Erste
Bank improved its solvency, K&H Bank and Raiffeisen Bank increased their
liquidity). All banks that belong to any of the selected financial conglomerates
(Erste Bank, K&H Bank, Raiffeisen Bank, and UniCredit Bank) are the banks
with the highest level of financial stability in the Hungarian banking sector, at
least in the last analysed years.

Table 18 Average values of aggregate financial stability index for Hungarian banks belonging to a financial group

Banks	2005–2007	2008–2012	2013–2018
Banking sector	0.48	0.47	0.49
Erste	0.48	0.48	0.51
Erste Group	0.58	0.61	0.68
K&H Bank	0.49	0.49	0.50
KBC Group	0.63	0.58	0.62
Raiffeisen	0.48	0.48	0.50
Raiffeisen Group	0.60	0.66	0.68
UniCredit	0.53	0.49	0.50
UniCredit Group	0.49	0.51	0.56

Source: Authors' calculations.

Table 19 Average values of aggregate financial stability index for Polish banks belonging to a financial group

Banks	2005–2007	2008–2012	2013–2018
Banking sector	0.49	0.47	0.47
Euro Bank	0.44	0.42	0.42
Soc. Generale Group	0.50	0.47	0.50

Source: Authors' calculations.

Table 19 (and Appendix 2) contains the results of the aggregate financial stability index for Polish banks. Only one bank belongs to financial conglomerate: Euro Bank was a member of Societe Generale Group in the analysed period. Financial stability of Euro Bank is the lowest among the analysed banks, the reason being very low efficiency, accompanied by extremely low liquidity in the last years. The indices for other banks were therefore calculated only on the basis of the index described in Table 7. Bank Gospodarstwa Krajowego and Deutsche Bank Polska reached the most favourable values of the index, as they are efficient and profitable.

If we look at the results for Romanian banks (Table 20, Appendix 2), the worst values were recorded by OTP Bank Romania, due to poor efficiency and liquidity. In 2015, we saw the merger through absorption of Millennium Bank by OTP Bank Romania and now OTP Bank belongs to nine SIFIs in Romania. On the contrary, Libra Internet Bank reached the best value of the index in the Romanian banking sector (very good financial stability is a result of excellent performance and sufficient liquidity and solvency). Focusing on banks that belong to a financial

Table 20 Average values of aggregate financial stability index for Romanian banks belonging to a financial group

Banks	2005–2007	2008–2012	2013–2018
Banking sector	0.48	0.47	0.46
Commerciala	0.51	0.48	0.50
Erste Group	0.58	0.61	0.68
BRD	0.48	0.47	0.46
Soc. Generale Group	0.50	0.47	0.50
Raiffeisen	0.48	0.47	0.48
Raiffeisen Group	0.60	0.66	0.68
UniCredit	0.47	0.45	0.43
UniCredit Group	0.49	0.51	0.56

Source: Authors' calculations.

Table 21 Average values of aggregate financial stability index for Serbian banks belonging to a financial group

Banks	2005–2007	2008–2012	2013–2018
Banking sector	0.51	0.49	0.48
Erste	0.47	0.47	0.46
Erste Group	0.58	0.61	0.68
Soc. Generale	0.46	0.44	0.43
Soc. Generale Group	0.50	0.47	0.50
Raiffeisen	0.50	0.52	0.52
Raiffeisen Group	0.60	0.66	0.68
UniCredit	0.50	0.46	0.47
UniCredit Group	0.49	0.51	0.56

Source: Authors' calculations.

conglomerate, Banca Comerciala Romana, BRD-Groupe Societe Generale, Raiffeisen, and UniCredit Bank must be mentioned. While Banca Comerciala Romana, belonging to Erste Group, performs well, other banks that are members of financial groups are less stable; their financial stability is average or slightly below average.

The Serbian banking sector (Table 21, Appendix 2) is the first one where we can see, at least in some years, also banks with excellent financial stability (there are indicated by green colour; the values of the index range between 0.7 and 1.0): Opportunity Banka in 2005 and 2006, JUBMES Banka in 2008. JUBMES Banka has excellent efficiency and profitability (both in terms of ROA and NIM), very good solvency and liquidity), as well as Opportunity Banka. We can see also banks whose financial stability is below standard, such as Vojvodjanska Banka in 2005, OTP Bank in 2010, and NLB Banka in 2011–12, mainly due to low efficiency. Erste Bank, Raiffeisen Banka, Societe Generale Banka, and UniCredit Bank, all belong to our chosen financial conglomerates. Among them, Raiffeisen Banka is the most financially stable, its lower efficiency is offset by higher solvency and liquidity. Financial stability of other banks belonging to financial groups is even below average for the Serbian banking sector.

In spite of the relatively low number of Slovak banks in the sample (Table 22, Appendix 2), three of them belong to any financial conglomerate: ČSOB, Slovenska sporitelna, and Tatrabanka. Tatrabanka, a member of Raiffeisen Group, reached the highest value of the aggregate index among Slovak banks. Its lower liquidity is compensated by good performance and solvency. However, financial stability of two other banks is above average for the Slovak banking sector. The most fragile Slovak bank is Primabanka, whose vulnerability is a result of low liquidity and solvency and below average efficiency.

Financial stability of most Slovenian banks can be marked as average (Table 23, Appendix 2). There are only two banks whose values of aggregate index are highlighted with yellow in some years: Gorenjska Banka and Nova Ljubljanska Banka. Their good efficiency and profitability are accompanied by an increase in liquidity in those particular years. Adiko Bank and Sberbank can be mentioned as representatives of more fragile banks; their fragility is again caused by very low liquidity (Adiko Bank) or efficiency (Sberbank). While calculating the aggregate index, the financial stability of the parent company was considered for three banks: SKB Banka and UniCredit Banka for the whole period, and Nova Ljubljanska Banka for only 2005–12. Financial stabilities of SKB Banka and UniCredit Banka are average.

Table 22 Average values of aggregate financial stability index for Slovak banks belonging to a financial group

Banks	2005–2007	2008–2012	2013–2018
Banking sector	0.47	0.46	0.46
Sporitelna	0.47	0.47	0.47
Erste Group	0.58	0.61	0.68
CSOB	0.47	0.50	0.48
KBC Group	0.63	0.58	0.62
Tatrabanka	0.52	0.53	0.51
Raiffeisen Group	0.60	0.66	0.68

Source: Authors' calculations.

Table 23 Average values of aggregate financial stability index for Slovenian banks belonging to a financial group

Banks	2005–2007	2008–2012	2013–2018
Banking sector	0.46	0.45	0.45
Ljubljanska	0.49	0.47	0.48
KBC Group	0.63	0.58	0.62
SKB	0.43	0.43	0.45
Soc. Generale Group	0.50	0.47	0.50
UniCredit	0.47	0.46	0.48
UniCredit Group	0.49	0.51	0.56

Source: Authors' calculations.

The results provided in Tables 14–23 showed that the financial stability of none of the CEE banks examined was poor. This should not be surprising, because all these banks operate for the whole analysed period.

5.2 Effect of the Affiliation with the Financial Conglomerate on the Financial Stability of Individual Banks and Banking Sectors

The aim of this Element is also to assess the effect of the parent company (financial conglomerate) on the financial stability of commercial banks and national financial sectors. To be able to assess the effect on national banking sectors, it is useful to focus also on the average values of the aggregate financial stability index for individual banking sectors and compare values of the index with and without incorporating the financial stability of parent companies. Table 24 and Appendix 3 present the average values for the aggregate financial stability index (for banks that belong to financial conglomerates, the financial stability of the parent company was considered).

On average, Serbian and Hungarian banking sectors reached the highest level of financial stability. Our results confirm the finding of Todorović et al. (2018), who concluded that the Serbian banking sector was isolated from market risks and that these risks do not pose a threat to stable operations of the banking sector. Moreover, Lukić et al. (2019) confirmed that Serbian banking sector, even with high level of NPLs ratio, was robust and solvent throughout crisis, since provisions for loan losses and capital adequacy were significantly above critical zone. No systematically important bank was in a need for capital injection, though some banks were winded up. Moreover, Kočišová (2015) stated that the financial stability in Hungary increased over the last ten years.

Table 24 Average values of aggregate financial stability index (financial stability of the parent company was incorporated).

Banks	2005–2007	2008–2012	2013–2018
Bosnian and Herzeg.	0.50	0.47	0.47
Bulgarian	0.48	0.46	0.47
Czech	0.49	0.48	0.48
Croatian	0.48	0.47	0.47
Hungarian	0.48	0.47	0.49
Polish	0.49	0.47	0.47
Romanian	0.49	0.47	0.46
Serbian	0.51	0.48	0.49
Slovak	0.47	0.46	0.46
Slovenian	0.46	0.44	0.45

Source: Authors' calculations.

On the contrary, the financial stability of Slovak and Slovenian banking sector is the lowest. It is in line with the results of Karkowska and Pawłowska (2017). However, the financial stability of all banking sectors can be marked as average or even very good in some years/banking sectors, although the slight decrease in the banking stability of all estimated banking sectors was probably connected with the impact of the financial crisis and European sovereign debt crisis that is in line with the previous studies (Miklaszewska et al., 2012; Capraru and Andries, 2015, or Bayar et al., 2021). Bayar et al. (2021) added that it affected the ability and remained at a low growth rate and at the same time they provoked Basel III regulations which have increased requirements for capital required. As stated by Kočišová et al. (2018), the increase in financial stability during the last years could be caused by the regulatory pressure, and increased demand for higher levels of core capital, as well as the expectation of the effects of new Basel III accords, which led to the increase in quality and quantity of equity capital. We can conclude that the group of CEE countries as a whole has no significant problem with banking stability.

If we do not incorporate the financial stability of parent companies into the aggregate financial stability index, we can see that the overall financial stability in all CEE banking sectors deteriorates (Table 25, Appendix 3). There are only two banking sectors where financial stability can be marked as very good: Serbian banking sector in 2007 and 2009, and Czech banking sector in 2005. However, the differences seem to be not so large, at least at a first glance. Therefore, to measure the impact of financial conglomerates on individual banking sectors, it could be useful to calculate the percentage change of the aggregate financial stability index after the inclusion of the financial stability of

Table 25 Average values of aggregate financial stability index (financial stability of the parent company was not incorporated)

Banks	2005–2007	2008–2012	2013–2018
Bosnian and Herzeg.	0.50	0.48	0.46
Bulgarian	0.48	0.46	0.47
Czech	0.49	0.48	0.47
Croatian	0.48	0.47	0.46
Hungarian	0.47	0.46	0.48
Polish	0.40	0.47	0.47
Romanian	0.48	0.46	0.46
Serbian	0.49	0.47	0.48
Slovak	0.51	0.48	0.48
Slovenian	0.45	0.45	0.45

Source: Authors' calculations.

the parent company. Results for individual relevant banks are recorded in Appendix 5, Table 26 provides the average values for the percentage change for particular banks in the relevant banking sectors (e.g., the average value for the Czech banking sector was calculated as an average value of percentage change for Česká spořitelna, ČSOB, Komerční banka, Raiffeisenbank, and UniCredit Bank, i.e., banks that are affiliated with selected financial groups).

Results confirm our previous conclusions that financial conglomerates contribute to increasing financial stability in all CEE banking sectors. The findings are line with Raykov and Silva-Buston (2020), who stated that banks in the financial group can enjoy the support of their parent when overcoming adverse shocks. Moreover, authors examined that banks that are part of a holding company were more stable than independent banks when affected by a negative shock; this evidence holds in terms of both individual and systemic risk. Their evidence suggested that there are no spillover effects within the financial group. The biggest influence can be seen in Slovak, Croatian, and Bosnian banking sectors. On the contrary, the lowest effect (but also positive) of financial conglomerates can be seen in Slovenian and Polish banking sectors. The low impact in these banking sectors can be connected with the low number of banks in the considered financial groups (see Section 3.4).

To be able to assess the effect of financial conglomerates on the financial stability of individual commercial banks, it is useful to focus again on the average values of the aggregate financial stability index and to compare values of the index with and without incorporating the financial stability of parent companies. The difference is that now we will classify our results according to

Table 26 Average values of the impact of financial stability of financial conglomerates on the aggregate financial stability index for individual banking sectors (in %)

Banks	2005–2007	2008–2012	2013–2018
Bosnian and Herzeg.	1.97	3.34	4.17
Bulgarian	1.17	2.22	2.90
Czech	1.50	1.80	2.65
Croatian	1.93	2.80	3.63
Hungarian	1.93	2.52	3.00
Polish	1.43	1.32	2.28
Romanian	1.37	2.32	3.38
Serbian	1.50	2.12	3.30
Slovak	4.73	5.52	6.75
Slovenian	1.73	1.62	1.63

Source: Authors' calculations.

Table 27 Average values of aggregate financial stability index for banks in the financial conglomerate (financial stability of the parent company was incorporated)

Banks	2005–2007	2008–2012	2013–2018
Erste	0.48	0.48	0.48
Soc. Generale	0.46	0.45	0.45
KBC	0.49	0.49	0.49
UniCredit	0.48	0.46	0.48
Raiffeisen	0.49	0.49	0.50

Source: Authors' calculations.

individual financial groups. Table 27 and Appendix 4 present the average values for the aggregate financial stability index for banks in financial conglomerates (financial stability of the parent company was considered). The average values were calculated for all banks belonging to the given financial conglomerate, regardless of the country in which they operate (e.g., the average value for the KBC Group was calculated as an average value of the aggregate index for United Bulgarian Bank, ČSOB, Komerční banka, K&H Bank, ČSOB Slovakia, and Nova Ljubljanska Banka, i.e., banks that belongs to the KBC Group).

Banks from KBC Group and Raiffeisen Group reached the highest financial stability during the whole analysed period. On the contrary, the lowest values of the index were recorded by banks belonging to Societe Generale Group.

Table 28 Average values of aggregate financial stability index for banks in the financial conglomerate (financial stability of the parent company was not incorporated)

Banks	2005–2007	2008–2012	2013–2018
Erste	0.47	0.46	0.46
Soc. Generale	0.46	0.45	0.44
KBC	0.47	0.47	0.48
UniCredit	0.48	0.46	0.46
Raiffeisen	0.47	0.47	0.47

Source: Authors' calculations.

Nevertheless, the differences between the minimum and maximum values are rather small, so we can conclude that the financial stability of all banks belonging to these selected financial conglomerates is (on average) quite similar.

If we do not incorporate the financial stability of parent companies into the aggregate financial stability index, we can see that the overall financial stability in all financial groups mostly deteriorates (Table 28, Appendix 4). This is the same effect as we could see for individual banking sectors. Financial stability of banks from all financial groups falls to the level 'average', which is indicated by the orange colour.

To be able to measure the impact of financial stability of parent companies on individual banks belonging to the chosen financial groups more precisely, we will again focus on the percentage change of the aggregate financial stability index after the inclusion of the financial stability of the parent company. Detailed results are provided in Appendix 5. Table 29 presents the average values for the percentage change for banks that are affiliated with a particular financial group.

Results for individual financial groups are not as straightforward as in the case of the whole banking sectors. We can see significant differences among financial groups. On average, in the case of UniCredit Group (in 2005 and 2008) and Societe Generale Group (in 2008), the financial stability of banks belonging to these groups deteriorated due to the worsening financial stability of the corresponding parent companies. Looking at more detailed data (Appendix 3), we can see that this problem appeared in several banks also in other years. Financial stability of the parent company lowered the financial stability of Komerční banka, BRD-Groupe Societe Generale, and Societe Generale Banka Srbija. In the case of Komerční banka, this effect lasted for more than half of the analysed period. Focusing on UniCredit Group, only banks

Table 29 Average values of the impact of financial stability of financial conglomerates on the aggregate financial stability index for individual financial groups (in %)

Banks	2005–2007	2008–2012	2013–2018
Erste	2.35	2.33	4.87
Soc. Generale	0.99	0.55	1.36
KBC	3.19	2.21	2.95
UniCredit	0.24	1.14	2.06
Raiffeisen	3.48	5.11	5.38

Source: Authors' calculations.

from Bosnia and Hercegovina did not experience the effect of deterioration of their financial stability due to the financial stability of their parent company. Banks operating in other countries (Bulgaria, Czechia, Croatia, Hungary, Romania, Serbia, and Slovenia) have encountered this influence at least once (but typically in 2005, 2006, and 2008).

This analysis covers the period 2005–18. This period was characterized by the global financial crisis. When we consider GDP, as the most common indicator for measuring economic activity, in CEE countries and in the EU, the economy grew between 2005 and 2007. From 2008 to 2013, the CEE economy was strongly affected by the financial crisis and GDP dropped. Between 2014 and 2018, the economy progressively recovered, with annual growth rates around +2 per cent. Therefore, the rest of the analysed period can be considered relatively stable. During the crisis period, especially in 2008, the effect of the affiliation with the financial conglomerate on bank stability is visible, and the difference between the individual financial conglomerates is most evident during the financial crisis. This result is in line with the previous studies. For example, Allen et al. (2017) concluded that there is no evidence that the parent banks' financial performance and situation are directly related to their lending behaviours in CEE countries during normal economic times. However, the fundamentals of the parent bank increased in significance during crisis periods. Moreover, De Haas and Van Lelyveld (2014) found that credit growth of banking groups slowed about twice as much relative to domestic banks during the global financial crisis, thus acting as a source of instability. De Haas and Van Lelyveld (2014) argued that parent organizations that experience a banking crisis in the home market can no longer support subsidiaries and that internal funding may even be sourced from subsidiaries to rescue the business activity of the parent organization in its home market.

To make a conclusion, we should keep in mind that our sample includes only banks whose market share is approximately 75 per cent of the corresponding banking sector. Regarding this limitation, we can conclude that the presence of financial conglomerates in CEE banking sectors mostly increases the financial stability of these banking sectors. However, this is especially true mainly for banks belonging to Erste Group and Raiffeisen Group. In the case of banks from UniCredit Group or Societe Generale Group, the effect of affiliation with the financial conglomerate may be completely opposite, at least in some years.

6 Conclusion

The aim of the Element was threefold. First, to estimate financial stability in CEE using the constructed aggregate financial stability index for individual commercial banks. Second, to incorporate the financial stability of the parent company into the index. Third, to assess the effect of the parent company (financial conglomerate) on the financial stability of commercial banks and national financial sectors.

The aggregate index was constructed as a weighted sum of the selected indicators. We considered three indicators of performance (ROA and NIM as profitability ratios, and the results of dynamic DEA as a measure of efficiency), two ratios of liquidity (share of liquid assets in total assets and share of loans to deposits), one ratio of solvency (level of capitalization), one ratio of credit risk (share of NPLs in total gross loans), and the financial stability of the parent company, where applicable. In the case of stand-alone banks, all four categories (performance, liquidity, solvency, and asset quality) had the same weights. For banks that belong to a financial conglomerate, we had lightly lowered the weights for these categories as it was necessary to incorporate the financial stability of the parent company.

We focused on the region of CEE countries, namely, on banks operating in Czechia, Slovakia, Hungary, Poland, Romania, Bulgaria, Croatia, Serbia, Bosnia and Herzegovina, and Slovenia, and five financial groups, particularly Erste Group, KBC Group, Raiffeisen Group, Societe Generale Group, and UniCredit Group. Market share of banks in our sample amounts around 75 per cent of the banking sector assets in individual countries. The fact that we focus on financial groups (and not directly on financial conglomerates) is a limitation of our research, as well as the fact due to the data availability, we could use only data on a yearly basis.

First, we have calculated the aggregate financial stability index for parent companies. Erste Group and Raiffeisen Group reached the highest financial stability, and the financial stability of Societe Generale was significantly lower.

Then, we assessed the financial stability of all banks in the sample. Financial stability of most banks is average or very good. A few banks reached excellent values of the index, and the financial stability of some other banks was below standard. None of the CEE banks examined had poor financial stability. As we focused only on banks that operate for the whole analysed period, our results are not surprising.

To assess the effect of the affiliation with the financial conglomerate on national banking sectors, we compared the average values of the aggregate financial stability index for individual banking sectors, calculated with and without incorporating the financial stability of parent companies. Serbian and Hungarian banking sector belong to the most financially stable; on the other hand, the financial stability of Slovak and Slovenian banking sector is lower. However, the group of CEE countries as a whole has no significant problem with banking fragility. The results showed that when we remove the influence of the parent company, the overall financial stability in all CEE banking sectors deteriorates. Calculated percentage change of the aggregate index with and without the impact of parent companies proved that financial conglomerates (on average) contributed to higher financial stability in all CEE banking sectors. The biggest effects were recorded in Slovak and Croatian banking sectors, the lowest effect in Slovenian and Polish banking sectors.

We used a similar approach to assess also the effect of financial conglomerate on the financial stability of individual commercial banks. Therefore, we compared the average values of the aggregate financial stability index calculated with and without incorporating the financial stability of parent companies, regardless of the country in which the banks operate. Banks from KBC Group and Raiffeisen Group reached the highest financial stability; the financial stability of banks belonging to Societe Generale was the lowest. Calculated percentage change of the aggregate index with and without the impact of parent companies showed that the impact of affiliation with a financial conglomerate on the financial stability of the bank differs among financial conglomerates. Financial stability of many banks belonging to UniCredit Group and Societe Generale Group deteriorated due to the worsening financial stability of the corresponding parent companies, at least in some years. In the case of Erste Group, KBC Group, and Raiffeisen Group, the financial stability of individual banks belonging to these financial groups is enhanced with the financial stability of the corresponding parent companies.

However, as our sample includes only banks whose market share is approximately 75 per cent of the particular banking sectors, our results could change by including other banks.

Our results have implications for regulators, policymakers, and bank managers. Although it seems that banks in CEE are not currently threatened by financial instability, regulators and policymakers in the CEE region should focus attention on this topic moreover in the context of the current pandemic situation. However, the pandemic period is a major challenge for policymakers and regulators as well as the bank managers. We can emphasize the recommendation of Ma Mateev et al. (2021), who stated that, on one side, all concerned authorities and regulators should take appropriate measures to sustain the economy by any means rather than accelerating the economic growth, although the post-Covid-19 period is not seen to expect a change in economic growth prospects (Schuknecht, 2022). Therefore, regulators responsible for banking sector stability should require a more disciplined approach in bank lending decisions and building a sufficient capital conservation' buffer to limit the impact of downside risk from depletion of capital buffers which can be significant during the pandemic. On the other side, this necessitates a more responsible behaviour on behalf of the bank managers when they develop their risky strategies. Furthermore, it has been found that banks in a financial group are more financially stable than individual banks. Nevertheless, a deeper analysis of these causes is needed. Financial groups are also associated with several risks, so it is appropriate to pay deeper attention to this topic from the regulators. In further research, the attention can be focused on the individual sub-indices of the composite banking stability index. Alternatively, further research can also focus on the determinants of the bank stability index, such as financial markets factors or the macroeconomic factors, which may be helpful in revealing potential bank fragility issues and thus highlighting potential bank risks to both bank managers and regulators. More detailed research may also reveal other areas of the impact of affiliation with the financial conglomerate on individual banks.

Moreover, the current and forthcoming period will be significantly influenced by the Covid-19 pandemic. Ellis et al. (2021) remind that global crises have highlighted the need for a better understanding of financial stability and regulation of the financial system. As some authors (e.g. Berger and Demirgüç-Kunt, 2021; Duan et al., 2021, or Park and Shin, 2021) started research in this area, the crisis period is a challenge for many researchers. The financial crisis of 2008–9 and the current Covid-19 pandemic have posed unprecedented challenges to the financial system (Rizwan et al., 2020). However, these two crises visibly differ. The financial crisis originated from the vulnerabilities in the global financial system, which spilled over into the real economy. The Covid-19 pandemic is a worldwide health emergency that, together with the containment measures, imposes a severe shock on the real economy and threatens to impair the financial system's stability (Buch, 2020). Therefore, future research may focus on bank stability during the crisis period.

Appendix 1: List of Banks

List of banks in the sample

Country	Abbreviation	Name of the bank
Bosnia and Herzegovina	Bosna Bank Int.	Bosna Bank International d.d.
	Hypo Alpe-Adria	Hypo Alpe-Adria-Bank a.d.
	Intesa Sanpaolo	Intesa Sanpaolo Banka d.d. Bosna I Hercegovina
	Investiciono-Komer.	Investiciono-Komercijalna Banka d.d. Zenica
	Komercijalno-Invest.	Komercijalno-Investiciona Banka d.d. Velika Kladusa
	NLB Banka	NLB Banka d.d.
	Razvojna banka	Razvojna banka a.d.
	Nova Banka	Nova Banka a.d. Banja Luka
	Raiffeisen	Raiffeisenbank d.d. Bosnia and Herzegovina
	Sberbank	Sberbank a.d. Banja Luka
	Sparkasse	Sparkasse Bank d.d.
	UniCredit BL	UniCredit Bank a.d. Banja Luka
	UniCredit	UniCredit Bank BA
	Union	Union Banka d.d. Sarajevo
	Vakufska	Vakufska Banka d.d. Sarajevo
	ZiraatBank	ZiraatBank BH d.d.
Bulgaria	Allianz	Allianz Bank Bulgaria AD-CB Allianz Bulgaria AD
	Bulg.-American	Bulgarian-American Credit Bank
	Central Cooper.	Central Cooperative Bank
	D Commerce	D Commerce Bank AD
	DSK Bank	DSK Bank
	Eurobank	Eurobank Bulgaria AD-Postbank
	First Investment	First Investment Bank AD
	Internat. Asset	International Asset Bank AD
	Investbank	Investbank Plc
	Municipal	Municipal Bank Plc
	Piraeus	Piraeus Bank Bulgaria AD
	Raiffeisen	Raiffeisenbank (Bulgaria) EAD
	SG Express	Societe Generale Expressbank

Appendix 1: List of Banks

(cont.)

Country	Abbreviation	Name of the bank
	TBI Bank	TBI Bank EAD
	Teximbank	Teximbank-PEB Texim AD
	UniCredit	UniCredit Bulbank AD
	United Bulg.	United Bulgarian Bank – UBB
Czechia	Sporitelna	Česká spořitelna
	CSOB	ČSOB
	Equabank	Equabank (Banco Popolare, IC banka)
	Expobank	Expobank (Bawag Bank, LBBW Bank)
	Hypotecni	Hypoteční banka
	JT banka	JT banka
	Komerční	Komerční banka
	Moneta	Moneta Money Bank (GE Money Bank)
	PPF banka	PPF banka
	Raiffeisen	Raiffeisenbank
	Sberbank	Sberbank (Volksbank)
	UniCredit	UniCredit Bank (HVB Bank)
	Wustenrot	Wüstenrot hypoteční banka
Croatia	BKS Bank	BKS Bank
	Croatia	Croatia Banka
	Erste	Erste & Steiermärkische Bank
	Hrvatska	Hrvatska Postanska Bank
	Istarska	Istarska Kreditna Bank Umag
	JT bank	JT bank Vaba
	Karlovacka	Karlovacka banka
	Kreditna	Kreditna Banka Zagreb
	OTP	OTP banka Hrvatska
	Partner	Partner Banka
	Podravska	Podravska Banka
	Privredna	Privredna Banka Zagreb
	Raiffeisen	Raiffeisenbank Austria
	Sberbank	Sberbank
	Slatinska	Slatinska Banka
	Zagrebacka	Zagrebacka Banka

(cont.)

Country	Abbreviation	Name of the bank
Hungary	Budapest	Budapest Bank Nyrt-Budapest Hitel-és Fejleszési Bank Nyrt
	CIB	CIB Bank Zrt
	Commerz	Commerzbank Zrt
	Erste	Erste Bank Hungary Zrt
	K&H	K&H Bank Zrt
	MKB	MKB Bank Zrt
	OTP	OTP Bank Plc
	Raiffeisen	Raiffeisen Bank Zrt
	Sberbank	Sberbank
	UniCredit	UniCredit Bank Hungary Zrt
Poland	Gospodar	Bank Gospodarstwa Krajowego
	Handlowy	Bank Handlowy w Warszawie SA
	Millennium	Bank Millennium SA
	Ochr. Srodow.	Bank Ochrony Srodowiska SA – BOS SA-Bank Ochrony Srodowiska Capital Group
	Kasa Opieki	Bank Polska Kasa Opieki SA-Bank Pekao
	Pols. Spoldz.	Bank Polskiej Spoldzielczosci
	Deutsche	Deutsche Bank Polska SA
	DNB Bank	DNB Bank Polska SA
	Euro Bank	Euro Bank SA
	Getin Noble	Getin Noble Bank SA
	ING Bank	ING Bank Śląski SA
	MBank Hip.	MBank Hipoteczny SA
	mBank	mBank SA
	Pekao Hip.	Pekao Bank Hipoteczny Sa
	PKO	PKO
	Raiffeisen	Raiffeisen Bank Polska SA
	SGB Bank	SGB Bank SA
Romania	Alpha Bank	Alpha Bank Romania
	Commerciala	Banca Comerciala Romana SA
	BRD	BRD-Groupe Societe Generale SA
	Libra	Libra Internet Bank SA
	OTP	OTP Bank Romania SA
	First Bank	First Bank
	Raiffeisen	Raiffeisen

(cont.)

Country	Abbreviation	Name of the bank
	Transilvania	Transilvania Bank-Banca Transilvania SA
	UniCredit	UniCredit Bank SA
Serbia	AIK	AIK Banka ad Nis
	Intesa	Banca Intesa ad Beograd
	Cr. Agricole	Credit Agricole Srbija a.d. Novi Sad
	Erste	Erste Bank a.d. Novi Sad
	Eurobank	Eurobank AD Beograd
	Halkabank	Halkabank AD Belgrade
	Adiko	ADIKO Bank
	JUBMES	JUBMES Banka AD Beograd
	Komercijalna	Komercijalna Banka AD Beograd
	Expobank	Expobank
	NLB	NLB Banka AD Beogra
	Opportunity	Opportunity Banka a.d. Novi Sad
	OTP	OTP Bank Serbia ad Novi Sad
	Postanska	Banka Poštanska
	Raiffeisen	Raiffeisen
	Sberbank	Sberbank Serbia a.d. Beograd
	Soc. Generale	Societe Generale Banka Srbija
	Srpska	Srpska Bank
	Telenor	Telenor Banka ad Beograd
	UniCredit	UniCredit Bank Serbia JSC
	Vojvodjanska	Vojvodjanska Banka AD, Novi Sad
Slovakia	CSOB	Československá Obchodna Banka
	OTP	OTP SK
	Postova	Postova banka
	Primabanka	Primabanka
	Sporitelna	Slovenska sporitelna
	Tatrabanka	Tatrabanka
	VUB	Vseobecna Uverova Banka
Slovenia	Abanka	Abanka Vipa
	Adiko	Adiko bank
	Intesa	Banka Intesa Sanpaolo
	Delavska	Delavska hranilnica dd Ljubljana

(cont.)

Country	Abbreviation	Name of the bank
	Dezelna	Dezelna
	Gorenjska	Gorenjska Banka d.d. Kranj
	Ljubljanska	NLB dd-Nova Ljubljanska Banka
	Kreditna	Nova Kreditna Banka Maribor
	Postna	Postna Banka Slovenije SL
	Sberbank	Sberbank
	SKB	SKB Banka SL
	UniCredit	UniCredit Banka Slovenija SL

Source: Authors' processing.

Appendix 2: Financial Stability of Individual Banks

Aggregate financial stability for financial conglomerates (parent companies)

Groups	05	06	07	08	09	10	11	12	13	14	15	16	17	18
Erste Group	0.58	0.58	0.58	0.58	0.63	0.65	0.60	0.60	0.61	0.59	0.68	0.73	0.73	0.73
Societe Generale	0.50	0.53	0.47	0.45	0.49	0.48	0.45	0.47	0.53	0.46	0.47	0.50	0.51	0.51
KBC Group	0.61	0.65	0.62	0.54	0.55	0.63	0.60	0.58	0.56	0.61	0.59	0.61	0.63	0.70
UniCredit Group	0.46	0.48	0.52	0.43	0.53	0.56	0.49	0.54	0.50	0.52	0.52	0.54	0.63	0.62
Raiffeisen Group	0.56	0.57	0.67	0.69	0.67	0.67	0.65	0.63	0.64	0.59	0.63	0.70	0.74	0.80

Aggregate financial stability for individual banks

Banks	05	06	07	08	09	10	11	12	13	14	15	16	17	18
Bosnia and Herzegovina														
Bosna Bank Int.	0.58	0.59	0.57	0.55	0.52	0.52	0.51	0.50	0.51	0.51	0.50	0.51	0.51	0.50
Hypo Alpe-Adria	0.43	0.42	0.42	0.39	0.41	0.40	0.43	0.44	0.46	0.48	0.46	0.45	0.47	0.48
Intesa Sanpaolo	0.46	0.45	0.44	0.42	0.42	0.43	0.42	0.42	0.42	0.42	0.42	0.43	0.44	0.43
Investiciono-Komer.	0.57	0.57	0.56	0.56	0.56	0.56	0.55	0.55	0.55	0.54	0.52	0.53	0.50	0.51
Komercijalno-Invest.	0.61	0.59	0.57	0.56	0.57	0.56	0.56	0.57	0.56	0.57	0.52	0.53	0.53	0.53
NLB Banka	0.45	0.44	0.44	0.43	0.42	0.42	0.43	0.42	0.42	0.42	0.43	0.44	0.45	0.46
Razvojna banka	0.44	0.44	0.46	0.46	0.45	0.44	0.44	0.44	0.44	0.45	0.45	0.46	0.47	0.49
Nova Banka	0.51	0.51	0.50	0.47	0.46	0.47	0.44	0.44	0.42	0.43	0.43	0.44	0.45	0.46
Raiffeisen	0.46	0.45	0.45	0.44	0.45	0.45	0.46	0.45	0.46	0.46	0.46	0.48	0.48	0.49
Sberbank	0.51	0.47	0.47	0.47	0.47	0.49	0.47	0.44	0.43	0.44	0.43	0.44	0.44	0.45
Sparkasse	0.48	0.50	0.49	0.47	0.47	0.47	0.44	0.43	0.43	0.43	0.44	0.45	0.45	0.45
UniCredit BL	0.42	0.44	0.45	0.42	0.44	0.44	0.44	0.44	0.44	0.44	0.44	0.45	0.46	0.47
UniCredit	0.44	0.44	0.45	0.41	0.43	0.44	0.43	0.44	0.44	0.45	0.44	0.45	0.48	0.47

Union	0.51	0.52	0.51	0.51	0.52	0.51	0.53	0.51	0.47	0.47	0.44	0.44	0.46	0.48
Vakufska	0.51	0.51	0.57	0.53	0.51	0.50	0.48	0.47	0.47	0.44	0.45	0.44	0.47	0.47
ZiraatBank	0.63	0.64	0.61	0.59	0.59	0.60	0.60	0.55	0.51	0.49	0.50	0.50	0.50	0.51
Bulgaria														
Allianz	0.47	0.45	0.43	0.41	0.42	0.42	0.43	0.42	0.42	0.43	0.43	0.45	0.47	0.46
Bulg.-American	0.53	0.54	0.54	0.54	0.55	0.53	0.53	0.51	0.51	0.50	0.50	0.48	0.49	0.50
Central Cooper.	0.43	0.43	0.46	0.44	0.43	0.43	0.43	0.43	0.43	0.44	0.42	0.44	0.47	0.47
D Commerce	0.55	0.54	0.53	0.50	0.50	0.51	0.48	0.47	0.47	0.48	0.48	0.49	0.50	0.51
DSK Bank	0.44	0.45	0.43	0.41	0.42	0.43	0.43	0.44	0.44	0.45	0.45	0.46	0.45	0.48
Eurobank	0.46	0.45	0.43	0.41	0.41	0.42	0.43	0.42	0.43	0.44	0.44	0.46	0.46	0.46
First Investment	0.40	0.40	0.40	0.40	0.39	0.39	0.39	0.39	0.39	0.40	0.40	0.42	0.42	0.42
Internat. Asset	0.45	0.43	0.43	0.40	0.42	0.41	0.41	0.41	0.40	0.40	0.41	0.43	0.43	0.42
Investbank	0.49	0.50	0.50	0.48	0.48	0.48	0.47	0.48	0.47	0.47	0.47	0.47	0.47	0.50
Municipal	0.53	0.52	0.53	0.52	0.50	0.51	0.51	0.51	0.51	0.51	0.49	0.49	0.49	0.53
Piraeus	0.45	0.44	0.45	0.44	0.44	0.44	0.45	0.46	0.49	0.49	0.45	0.49	0.49	0.49
Raiffeisen	0.50	0.52	0.52	0.52	0.51	0.52	0.52	0.51	0.51	0.52	0.52	0.52	0.52	0.53

(cont.)

Banks	05	06	07	08	09	10	11	12	13	14	15	16	17	18
SG Express	0.45	0.44	0.42	0.41	0.41	0.41	0.42	0.41	0.42	0.41	0.41	0.42	0.44	0.43
TBI Bank	0.50	0.51	0.50	0.50	0.48	0.50	0.55	0.51	0.51	0.52	0.54	0.56	0.57	0.60
Teximbank	0.56	0.57	0.57	0.56	0.56	0.53	0.51	0.53	0.52	0.52	0.49	0.52	0.52	0.52
UniCredit	0.48	0.48	0.46	0.45	0.46	0.47	0.46	0.46	0.46	0.45	0.45	0.46	0.49	0.51
United Bulg.	0.44	0.44	0.42	0.40	0.40	0.41	0.42	0.43	0.44	0.45	0.44	0.45	0.48	0.46
Czechia														
Sporitelna	0.49	0.49	0.48	0.49	0.50	0.51	0.49	0.49	0.49	0.49	0.50	0.51	0.50	0.48
CSOB	0.51	0.50	0.51	0.48	0.49	0.49	0.49	0.49	0.49	0.51	0.51	0.50	0.49	0.50
Equabank	0.67	0.67	0.64	0.55	0.52	0.54	0.54	0.48	0.46	0.48	0.47	0.46	0.50	0.51
Expobank	0.50	0.49	0.47	0.48	0.48	0.48	0.48	0.47	0.47	0.47	0.46	0.47	0.53	0.53
Hypotecni	0.46	0.47	0.46	0.47	0.48	0.48	0.48	0.48	0.47	0.47	0.47	0.47	0.47	0.46
JT banka	0.50	0.49	0.47	0.47	0.49	0.48	0.48	0.49	0.49	0.48	0.50	0.51	0.52	0.51
Komercni	0.52	0.51	0.49	0.49	0.49	0.49	0.48	0.48	0.49	0.48	0.48	0.48	0.48	0.48
Moneta	0.50	0.49	0.47	0.46	0.46	0.46	0.47	0.47	0.47	0.49	0.48	0.46	0.46	0.43
PPF banka	0.52	0.51	0.54	0.54	0.53	0.52	0.52	0.52	0.50	0.50	0.48	0.50	0.52	0.52

Raiffeisen	0.49	0.48	0.49	0.49	0.49	0.49	0.49	0.49	0.49	0.49	0.49	0.49	0.51	0.51	0.49
Sberbank	0.41	0.42	0.42	0.42	0.41	0.41	0.41	0.42	0.41	0.42	0.42	0.42	0.41	0.42	0.41
UniCredit	0.48	0.48	0.49	0.48	0.48	0.48	0.48	0.49	0.48	0.48	0.48	0.48	0.49	0.51	0.50
Wustenrot	0.50	0.41	0.34	0.45	0.45	0.45	0.45	0.45	0.45	0.45	0.45	0.45	0.45	0.45	0.45
Croatia															
BKS Bank	0.52	0.52	0.52	0.50	0.50	0.48	0.49	0.50	0.50	0.50	0.49	0.49	0.46	0.45	0.49
Croatia	0.50	0.49	0.49	0.49	0.49	0.48	0.47	0.47	0.46	0.45	0.45	0.46	0.46	0.45	0.49
Erste	0.47	0.47	0.48	0.48	0.47	0.47	0.46	0.46	0.47	0.47	0.47	0.48	0.48	0.48	0.49
Hrvatska	0.51	0.47	0.47	0.45	0.44	0.44	0.44	0.44	0.42	0.42	0.44	0.46	0.46	0.47	0.47
Istarska	0.49	0.48	0.47	0.46	0.46	0.47	0.45	0.45	0.44	0.44	0.46	0.46	0.47	0.47	0.49
JT bank	0.51	0.47	0.50	0.47	0.47	0.47	0.46	0.47	0.48	0.48	0.47	0.48	0.48	0.48	0.51
Karlovacka	0.45	0.47	0.46	0.44	0.41	0.40	0.41	0.41	0.40	0.43	0.45	0.45	0.45	0.45	0.46
Kreditna	0.50	0.52	0.48	0.47	0.47	0.47	0.46	0.44	0.44	0.44	0.45	0.45	0.45	0.47	0.50
OTP	0.43	0.43	0.43	0.42	0.42	0.41	0.42	0.42	0.41	0.42	0.41	0.43	0.43	0.48	0.43
Partner	0.48	0.47	0.47	0.46	0.47	0.47	0.47	0.46	0.46	0.45	0.45	0.47	0.47	0.45	0.49
Podravska	0.48	0.44	0.44	0.45	0.45	0.44	0.43	0.44	0.44	0.43	0.44	0.44	0.44	0.46	0.48

(cont.)

Banks	05	06	07	08	09	10	11	12	13	14	15	16	17	18
Privredna	0.49	0.48	0.51	0.49	0.50	0.49	0.50	0.51	0.49	0.50	0.50	0.50	0.50	0.50
Raiffeisen	0.48	0.47	0.47	0.47	0.50	0.48	0.48	0.48	0.48	0.47	0.47	0.48	0.49	0.52
Sberbank	0.49	0.47	0.49	0.48	0.48	0.51	0.51	0.48	0.46	0.45	0.43	0.47	0.50	0.50
Slatinska	0.50	0.49	0.49	0.49	0.49	0.49	0.49	0.46	0.46	0.46	0.46	0.46	0.47	0.49
Zagrebacka	0.48	0.49	0.50	0.48	0.50	0.49	0.49	0.49	0.49	0.49	0.49	0.50	0.52	0.52
Hungary														
Budapest	0.44	0.43	0.42	0.41	0.40	0.41	0.42	0.46	0.47	0.46	0.46	0.45	0.44	0.43
CIB	0.46	0.47	0.46	0.45	0.46	0.46	0.46	0.46	0.46	0.48	0.49	0.50	0.50	0.50
Commerz	0.50	0.49	0.49	0.48	0.48	0.48	0.48	0.50	0.49	0.50	0.49	0.48	0.49	0.49
Erste	0.48	0.48	0.48	0.47	0.49	0.48	0.48	0.49	0.49	0.49	0.50	0.52	0.52	0.51
K&H	0.48	0.49	0.50	0.48	0.49	0.49	0.49	0.49	0.50	0.49	0.50	0.51	0.51	0.51
MKB	0.47	0.47	0.47	0.47	0.47	0.46	0.45	0.47	0.47	0.47	0.45	0.44	0.52	0.52
OTP	0.50	0.51	0.50	0.50	0.50	0.50	0.50	0.50	0.50	0.51	0.51	0.51	0.51	0.52
Raiffeisen	0.48	0.48	0.49	0.48	0.48	0.48	0.48	0.47	0.47	0.50	0.49	0.51	0.52	0.52
Sberbank	0.43	0.43	0.42	0.42	0.41	0.41	0.39	0.42	0.44	0.44	0.46	0.46	0.48	0.49
UniCredit	0.53	0.53	0.52	0.50	0.52	0.48	0.47	0.49	0.47	0.50	0.50	0.50	0.51	0.53

Poland

Gospodar	0.54	0.52	0.53	0.53	0.49	0.49	0.50	0.50	0.51	0.50	0.50	0.46	0.46	0.48
Handlowy	0.51	0.51	0.51	0.49	0.51	0.50	0.48	0.49	0.49	0.50	0.49	0.48	0.48	0.53
Millennium	0.49	0.49	0.47	0.47	0.46	0.46	0.47	0.46	0.46	0.47	0.46	0.46	0.46	0.50
Ochr. Srodow.	0.45	0.47	0.47	0.46	0.45	0.45	0.45	0.46	0.45	0.45	0.45	0.45	0.46	0.49
Kasa Opieki	0.50	0.50	0.49	0.49	0.49	0.49	0.48	0.49	0.48	0.49	0.48	0.47	0.47	0.49
Pols. Spoldz.	0.46	0.46	0.51	0.46	0.45	0.45	0.45	0.45	0.44	0.44	0.45	0.45	0.45	0.49
Deutsche	0.54	0.57	0.53	0.50	0.58	0.57	0.59	0.53	0.46	0.47	0.46	0.46	0.46	0.51
DNB Bank	0.48	0.48	0.47	0.46	0.45	0.45	0.45	0.46	0.47	0.47	0.47	0.47	0.47	0.48
Euro Bank	0.43	0.46	0.44	0.44	0.41	0.42	0.42	0.41	0.42	0.41	0.40	0.42	0.42	0.42
Getin Noble	0.62	0.62	0.53	0.48	0.46	0.46	0.46	0.46	0.45	0.46	0.45	0.46	0.45	0.46
ING Bank	0.51	0.50	0.51	0.48	0.48	0.46	0.46	0.47	0.47	0.47	0.46	0.46	0.46	0.48
MBank Hip.	0.45	0.46	0.45	0.45	0.45	0.45	0.45	0.45	0.45	0.45	0.45	0.45	0.45	0.46
mBank	0.49	0.48	0.47	0.46	0.46	0.46	0.46	0.47	0.47	0.47	0.47	0.48	0.48	0.50
Pekao Hip.	0.47	0.47	0.47	0.47	0.47	0.47	0.47	0.48	0.48	0.47	0.47	0.47	0.48	0.47
PKO	0.51	0.50	0.49	0.48	0.49	0.49	0.49	0.49	0.49	0.48	0.48	0.48	0.48	0.50

(cont.)

Banks	05	06	07	08	09	10	11	12	13	14	15	16	17	18
Raiffeisen	0.49	0.50	0.50	0.50	0.50	0.51	0.50	0.49	0.49	0.47	0.49	0.50	0.50	0.51
SGB Bank	0.47	0.49	0.47	0.46	0.46	0.45	0.45	0.46	0.45	0.45	0.45	0.45	0.45	0.45
Romania														
Alpha Bank	0.52	0.51	0.49	0.49	0.48	0.47	0.47	0.47	0.47	0.46	0.47	0.49	0.49	0.50
Commerciala	0.51	0.51	0.50	0.50	0.49	0.49	0.48	0.46	0.49	0.48	0.50	0.50	0.50	0.51
BRD	0.49	0.48	0.46	0.47	0.48	0.48	0.48	0.46	0.45	0.44	0.45	0.46	0.47	0.50
Libra	0.52	0.52	0.51	0.52	0.53	0.55	0.54	0.53	0.51	0.50	0.49	0.49	0.50	0.51
OTP	0.49	0.45	0.42	0.39	0.40	0.40	0.40	0.40	0.39	0.39	0.39	0.40	0.40	0.41
First Bank	0.47	0.45	0.44	0.43	0.42	0.42	0.44	0.45	0.42	0.42	0.44	0.45	0.47	0.48
Raiffeisen	0.48	0.47	0.48	0.48	0.46	0.47	0.46	0.47	0.46	0.48	0.47	0.48	0.48	0.49
Transilvania	0.50	0.50	0.49	0.49	0.49	0.47	0.46	0.47	0.47	0.47	0.48	0.48	0.48	0.52
UniCredit	0.48	0.47	0.47	0.45	0.46	0.46	0.44	0.43	0.42	0.42	0.42	0.42	0.43	0.47
Serbia														
AIK	0.60	0.57	0.53	0.55	0.52	0.50	0.51	0.51	0.50	0.49	0.48	0.50	0.52	0.52
Intesa	0.42	0.44	0.46	0.44	0.43	0.43	0.46	0.46	0.46	0.48	0.47	0.48	0.49	0.49

Cr. Agricole	0.45	0.41	0.41	0.44	0.42	0.42	0.41	0.41	0.40	0.42	0.42	0.41	0.43
Erste	0.46	0.45	0.50	0.48	0.48	0.46	0.47	0.47	0.47	0.47	0.46	0.46	0.46
Eurobank	0.44	0.47	0.48	0.50	0.50	0.46	0.44	0.46	0.46	0.47	0.45	0.45	0.47
Halkabank	0.56	0.57	0.51	0.47	0.47	0.46	0.44	0.46	0.45	0.46	0.45	0.44	0.46
Adiko	0.49	0.52	0.53	0.54	0.50	0.49	0.51	0.50	0.49	0.48	0.49	0.51	0.51
JUBMES	0.61	0.67	0.68	0.79	0.65	0.62	0.63	0.63	0.59	0.55	0.56	0.54	0.54
Komercijalna	0.43	0.45	0.42	0.44	0.44	0.44	0.45	0.46	0.45	0.45	0.43	0.45	0.51
Expobank	0.47	0.48	0.50	0.49	0.51	0.50	0.48	0.50	0.50	0.48	0.47	0.49	0.53
NLB	0.48	0.46	0.47	0.43	0.41	0.43	0.39	0.39	0.41	0.46	0.47	0.46	0.48
Opportunity	0.75	0.75	0.61	0.56	0.53	0.52	0.51	0.51	0.51	0.51	0.52	0.54	0.55
OTP	0.61	0.49	0.51	0.46	0.43	0.39	0.45	0.46	0.50	0.50	0.49	0.52	0.50
Postanska	0.43	0.50	0.48	0.53	0.51	0.52	0.52	0.42	0.41	0.47	0.45	0.48	0.49
Raiffeisen	0.47	0.49	0.53	0.53	0.53	0.52	0.50	0.50	0.51	0.52	0.52	0.52	0.51
Sberbank	0.51	0.55	0.54	0.53	0.51	0.51	0.50	0.50	0.51	0.52	0.50	0.52	0.53
Soc. Generale	0.43	0.46	0.48	0.47	0.45	0.42	0.43	0.43	0.43	0.43	0.43	0.43	0.44
Srpska	0.59	0.63	0.60	0.59	0.55	0.53	0.55	0.52	0.49	0.43	0.54	0.56	0.56

(cont.)

Banks	05	06	07	08	09	10	11	12	13	14	15	16	17	18
Telenor	0.47	0.52	0.54	0.54	0.52	0.48	0.47	0.46	0.59	0.63	0.51	0.49	0.50	0.52
UniCredit	0.49	0.50	0.52	0.48	0.47	0.45	0.46	0.46	0.46	0.46	0.45	0.46	0.48	0.49
Vojvodjanska	0.36	0.42	0.47	0.47	0.47	0.43	0.44	0.44	0.43	0.43	0.44	0.44	0.44	0.45
Slovakia														
CSOB	0.45	0.46	0.51	0.52	0.49	0.50	0.49	0.48	0.48	0.48	0.48	0.47	0.48	0.48
OTP	0.43	0.44	0.44	0.43	0.43	0.43	0.44	0.43	0.42	0.44	0.44	0.44	0.46	0.46
Postova	0.47	0.48	0.48	0.46	0.44	0.42	0.42	0.43	0.43	0.44	0.44	0.48	0.52	0.51
Primabanka	0.43	0.43	0.43	0.41	0.41	0.40	0.41	0.42	0.42	0.42	0.43	0.43	0.42	0.41
Sporitelna	0.48	0.47	0.47	0.46	0.47	0.48	0.48	0.47	0.47	0.46	0.47	0.47	0.47	0.47
Tatrabanka	0.49	0.53	0.53	0.54	0.52	0.52	0.52	0.53	0.52	0.52	0.51	0.51	0.51	0.51
VUB	0.46	0.46	0.46	0.46	0.46	0.45	0.46	0.46	0.46	0.46	0.45	0.44	0.46	0.45
Slovenia														
Abanka	0.48	0.47	0.47	0.47	0.47	0.46	0.45	0.45	0.45	0.47	0.47	0.49	0.48	0.48
Adiko	0.46	0.45	0.42	0.43	0.42	0.40	0.42	0.41	0.41	0.40	0.41	0.43	0.45	0.46
Intesa	0.42	0.43	0.42	0.42	0.43	0.42	0.43	0.43	0.43	0.44	0.45	0.45	0.45	0.46

Delavska	0.46	0.46	0.47	0.47	0.45	0.45	0.45	0.45	0.45	0.45	0.45	0.46	0.47	0.44
Dezelna	0.47	0.46	0.46	0.43	0.43	0.44	0.43	0.42	0.41	0.41	0.41	0.42	0.42	0.43
Gorenjska	0.52	0.51	0.50	0.50	0.49	0.49	0.49	0.48	0.48	0.48	0.48	0.48	0.49	0.50
Ljubljanska	0.50	0.49	0.48	0.47	0.47	0.47	0.46	0.47	0.47	0.46	0.48	0.48	0.48	0.50
Kreditna	0.45	0.42	0.42	0.41	0.41	0.42	0.43	0.42	0.44	0.44	0.48	0.46	0.46	0.45
Postna	0.44	0.47	0.46	0.46	0.45	0.46	0.46	0.46	0.45	0.45	0.45	0.49	0.48	0.48
Sberbank	0.41	0.45	0.44	0.42	0.43	0.43	0.42	0.43	0.42	0.42	0.42	0.43	0.43	0.44
SKB	0.44	0.43	0.43	0.43	0.43	0.43	0.42	0.43	0.44	0.44	0.45	0.45	0.45	0.44
UniCredit	0.47	0.48	0.47	0.46	0.47	0.46	0.46	0.46	0.48	0.46	0.47	0.47	0.49	0.49

Source: Authors' calculations.

Appendix 3: Financial Stability of Individual Banking Sectors

Average values of aggregate financial stability index (financial stability of the parent company was incorporated)

Banks	05	06	07	08	09	10	11	12	13	14	15	16	17	18
Bosnian and Herzeg.	0.50	0.50	0.50	0.48	0.48	0.48	0.48	0.47	0.47	0.47	0.46	0.47	0.47	0.48
Bulgarian	0.48	0.48	0.47	0.46	0.46	0.46	0.46	0.46	0.46	0.46	0.46	0.47	0.48	0.49
Czech	0.50	0.49	0.48	0.48	0.48	0.48	0.48	0.48	0.48	0.48	0.48	0.48	0.49	0.48
Croatian	0.49	0.48	0.48	0.47	0.47	0.47	0.46	0.46	0.45	0.46	0.45	0.46	0.48	0.49
Hungarian	0.48	0.48	0.47	0.47	0.47	0.47	0.46	0.47	0.48	0.49	0.48	0.49	0.50	0.50
Polish	0.49	0.50	0.49	0.48	0.47	0.47	0.47	0.47	0.47	0.46	0.46	0.46	0.46	0.48
Romanian	0.50	0.48	0.48	0.47	0.47	0.47	0.46	0.46	0.45	0.45	0.46	0.46	0.47	0.49
Serbian	0.50	0.51	0.51	0.51	0.49	0.47	0.48	0.47	0.48	0.48	0.48	0.48	0.49	0.50
Slovak	0.46	0.47	0.47	0.47	0.46	0.46	0.46	0.46	0.46	0.46	0.46	0.46	0.47	0.47
Slovenian	0.46	0.46	0.45	0.45	0.45	0.44	0.44	0.44	0.44	0.45	0.45	0.46	0.46	0.46

Source: Authors' calculations.

Average values of aggregate financial stability index (financial stability of the parent company was not incorporated)

Banks	05	06	07	08	09	10	11	12	13	14	15	16	17	18
Bosnian and Herzeg.	0.50	0.50	0.50	0.48	0.48	0.48	0.47	0.47	0.46	0.46	0.46	0.46	0.47	0.47
Bulgarian	0.48	0.48	0.47	0.46	0.46	0.46	0.46	0.46	0.46	0.46	0.46	0.47	0.48	0.48
Czech	0.50	0.49	0.48	0.48	0.48	0.48	0.48	0.47	0.47	0.47	0.47	0.47	0.48	0.47
Croatian	0.48	0.48	0.48	0.47	0.47	0.47	0.46	0.46	0.45	0.45	0.45	0.46	0.47	0.49
Hungarian	0.47	0.47	0.47	0.46	0.47	0.46	0.46	0.47	0.47	0.48	0.48	0.48	0.49	0.49
Polish	0.49	0.49	0.48	0.48	0.47	0.47	0.47	0.47	0.47	0.46	0.46	0.46	0.46	0.48
Romanian	0.49	0.48	0.47	0.47	0.46	0.46	0.46	0.45	0.45	0.45	0.45	0.46	0.46	0.48
Serbian	0.47	0.49	0.51	0.49	0.50	0.46	0.46	0.46	0.46	0.47	0.47	0.48	0.49	0.49
Slovak	0.50	0.51	0.51	0.51	0.49	0.47	0.48	0.47	0.48	0.48	0.47	0.48	0.49	0.49
Slovenian	0.45	0.45	0.46	0.45	0.45	0.45	0.45	0.45	0.45	0.45	0.45	0.45	0.46	0.46

Source: Authors' calculations.

Appendix 4: Financial Stability of Banks in Financial Conglomerates

Average values of aggregate financial stability index for banks in the financial conglomerate (financial stability of the parent company was incorporated)

Banks	05	06	07	08	09	10	11	12	13	14	15	16	17	18
Erste	0.48	0.48	0.49	0.48	0.48	0.48	0.47	0.47	0.47	0.47	0.48	0.48	0.48	0.48
Soc. Generale	0.46	0.47	0.46	0.46	0.45	0.44	0.45	0.44	0.44	0.44	0.44	0.45	0.45	0.45
KBC	0.49	0.48	0.50	0.49	0.49	0.49	0.48	0.48	0.49	0.50	0.49	0.49	0.49	0.48
UniCredit	0.48	0.48	0.48	0.46	0.47	0.46	0.46	0.46	0.46	0.46	0.46	0.46	0.49	0.49
Raiffeisen	0.48	0.49	0.49	0.49	0.49	0.49	0.49	0.49	0.49	0.50	0.49	0.50	0.50	0.51

Source: Authors' calculations.

Average values of aggregate financial stability index for banks in the financial conglomerate (financial stability of the parent company was not incorporated).

Banks	05	06	07	08	09	10	11	12	13	14	15	16	17	18
Erste	0.47	0.47	0.48	0.47	0.46	0.46	0.46	0.45	0.46	0.46	0.46	0.46	0.46	0.46
Soc. Generale	0.46	0.46	0.46	0.46	0.45	0.44	0.45	0.44	0.43	0.44	0.44	0.44	0.44	0.45
KBC	0.47	0.47	0.48	0.49	0.48	0.48	0.47	0.47	0.47	0.47	0.48	0.48	0.48	0.48
UniCredit	0.48	0.48	0.48	0.46	0.46	0.45	0.46	0.45	0.45	0.46	0.45	0.46	0.47	0.48
Raiffeisen	0.47	0.47	0.47	0.47	0.47	0.47	0.46	0.47	0.47	0.48	0.47	0.47	0.47	0.47

Source: Authors' calculations.

Appendix 5: Impact of Financial Conglomerates on Financial Stability

Average values of the impact of financial stability of financial conglomerates on the aggregate financial stability index for individual banking sectors (in %)

Banks	05	06	07	08	09	10	11	12	13	14	15	16	17	18
Bosnian and Herzeg.	1.3	1.7	2.9	2.5	3.7	4.2	3.0	3.5	3.1	2.8	3.7	4.3	5.4	5.7
Bulgarian	0.4	0.6	2.5	1.6	2.7	2.6	1.8	2.4	2.0	1.7	2.1	2.9	3.9	4.8
Czech	1.0	1.6	1.9	1.2	1.9	2.4	1.7	1.8	1.8	1.5	2.0	2.7	3.5	4.4
Croatian	1.5	1.7	2.6	2.2	2.9	3.5	2.6	2.8	2.5	2.2	3.4	4.0	4.9	4.8
Hungarian	1.5	1.9	2.4	1.8	2.4	3.4	2.5	2.5	2.2	1.9	2.6	3.0	3.9	4.4
Polish	1.9	1.6	0.8	0.4	2.1	1.7	0.8	1.6	3.1	1.4	1.8	2.2	2.6	2.6
Romanian	0.8	1.4	1.9	1.5	2.6	2.8	2.1	2.6	2.8	2.1	2.9	3.7	4.6	4.2
Serbian	1.7	1.6	1.2	1.0	2.3	3.0	1.9	2.4	2.6	1.7	2.7	3.6	4.5	4.7
Slovak	2.8	6.2	5.2	4.7	5.6	6.1	5.7	5.5	5.6	5.9	6.6	7.2	7.4	7.8
Slovenian	1.3	2.0	1.9	0.6	1.6	2.5	1.6	1.8	1.8	0.8	0.9	1.3	2.5	2.5

Source: Authors' calculations.

Impact of financial stability of financial conglomerates on aggregate financial stability index for individual banks (according to financial group; in %)

Banks	05	06	07	08	09	10	11	12	13	14	15	16	17	18
Erste Group														
BA Sparkasse			2.0	2.7	3.8	4.6	4.2	4.5	4.7	4.1	6.2	7.3	7.3	7.4
CZ Sporitelna	2.2	2.2	2.2	2.1	3.0	3.3	2.7	2.7	2.7	2.3	4.0	5.1	5.2	6.0
HR Erste	2.9	2.8	2.2	2.4	4.1	4.6	3.7	3.6	3.5	2.9	5.2	6.2	6.3	5.9
HU Erste	2.4	2.4	2.4	2.6	3.4	4.0	2.7	2.6	2.6	2.2	4.1	4.7	4.8	5.0
RO Commerciala	1.6	1.5	1.7	1.9	3.2	3.9	3.0	3.4	2.7	2.6	4.2	5.2	5.2	5.0
RS Erste	3.1	3.4	1.6	2.5	3.7	4.4	3.0	3.3	3.7	3.0	5.3	6.6	6.9	7.3
SK Sporitelna	2.5	2.7	2.5	2.9	4.0	4.0	3.0	3.2	3.5	3.2	5.3	6.4	6.4	6.5
Mean	2.5	2.5	2.1	2.4	3.6	4.1	3.2	3.3	3.3	2.9	4.9	5.9	6.0	6.2
KBC Group														
BG United Bulg.													3.7	5.9
CZ CSOB	2.3	3.3	2.3	1.5	1.4	3.0	2.6	2.1	1.6	2.3	1.9	2.5	3.3	4.7
HU K&H	3.0	3.8	2.7	1.4	1.3	3.1	2.6	1.9	1.5	2.7	2.1	2.3	2.9	4.1
SK CSOB	4.2	4.9	2.3	0.4	1.4	3.0	2.6	2.1	1.9	3.0	2.8	3.3	3.8	5.1
SL Ljubljanska	2.6	3.6	3.3	1.7	2.1	4.0	3.4	2.6						
Mean	3.0	3.9	2.7	1.3	1.6	3.3	2.8	2.2	1.7	2.7	2.3	2.7	3.4	4.9

Raiffeisen Group

BA Raiffeisen	2.6	3.1	5.8	6.7	5.9	5.8	5.0	4.6	4.5	3.3	4.2	5.5	6.3	7.8
BG Raiffeisen	1.3	1.2	3.4	3.8	3.6	3.1	3.0	2.8	2.8	1.6	2.4	3.9	4.9	6.0
CZ Raiffeisen	1.6	2.0	4.5	4.6	4.2	4.3	3.9	3.4	3.4	2.3	3.3	4.4	5.2	7.6
HR Raiffeisen	2.0	2.4	5.1	5.3	3.9	4.5	4.3	3.8	3.7	2.9	4.1	5.1	5.9	6.5
HU Raiffeisen	2.0	2.2	4.5	5.0	4.7	4.6	4.2	4.1	4.0	2.1	3.5	4.2	5.2	6.5
RO Raiffeisen	1.9	2.3	4.6	5.0	5.2	5.0	4.7	4.1	4.4	2.6	4.0	5.5	6.6	7.7
RS Raiffeisen	2.4	1.7	3.1	3.3	3.1	3.3	3.4	3.0	2.8	1.5	2.6	4.3	5.2	6.8
SK Tatrabanka	1.8	11.0	10.8	10.7	11.3	11.3	11.4	11.1	11.4	11.5	11.8	11.8	12.0	11.8
Mean	2.0	3.2	5.3	5.6	5.2	5.2	4.9	4.6	4.6	3.5	4.5	5.6	6.4	7.6

Societe Generale Group

CZ Komercni	−0.4	0.4	−0.3	−0.8	−0.1	−0.2	−0.6	−0.3	0.9	−0.4	−0.3	0.4	0.9	0.8
PL Euro Bank	1.9	1.6	0.8	0.4	2.1	1.7	0.8	1.6	3.1	1.4	1.8	2.2	2.6	2.6
RO BRD	0.4	1.3	0.2	−0.3	0.3	−0.1	−0.6	0.2	2.2	0.5	0.6	0.8	1.1	0.4
RS Soc. Generale	2.0	1.7	−0.1	−0.3	1.0	1.7	0.6	1.4	2.8	1.0	1.1	1.6	2.3	1.9
SL Soc. Generale	1.6	2.5	1.2	0.7	1.4	1.3	0.8	1.1	2.6	0.5	0.6	1.2	1.7	2.0
Mean	1.1	1.5	0.4	−0.1	0.9	0.9	0.2	0.8	2.3	0.6	0.8	1.2	1.7	1.5

UniCredit Group

BA UniCredit BL	1.0	0.9	1.7	0.3	2.5	3.2	1.3	2.5	1.5	2.0	2.2	2.3	4.2	3.7
BA UniCredit	0.4	0.9	1.9	0.3	2.8	3.2	1.3	2.5	1.6	1.8	2.1	2.1	3.8	3.8
BG UniCredit	−0.5	0.1	1.6	−0.5	1.8	2.1	0.5	1.9	1.1	1.9	1.9	2.0	3.2	2.6
CZ UniCredit	−0.6	−0.0	0.8	−1.2	1.0	1.5	0.2	1.3	0.5	1.0	0.9	1.1	2.8	2.8

(cont.)

Banks	05	06	07	08	09	10	11	12	13	14	15	16	17	18
HR Zagrebacka	−0.6	−0.1	0.5	−1.3	0.9	1.4	−0.1	1.0	0.4	0.7	0.8	0.7	2.5	2.1
HU UniCredit	−1.4	−0.9	0.1	−1.7	0.3	1.8	0.4	1.2	0.7	0.6	0.6	0.8	2.8	2.0
RO UniCredit	−0.5	0.3	1.2	−0.5	1.9	2.3	1.3	2.9	2.1	2.6	2.8	3.2	5.5	3.7
RS UniCredit	−0.8	−0.4	0.2	−1.3	1.6	2.6	0.6	1.9	1.2	1.4	1.8	1.8	3.5	2.9
SL UniCredit	−0.3	−0.1	1.2	−0.7	1.5	2.4	0.6	1.8	1.0	1.1	1.3	1.4	3.3	3.1
Mean	−0.4	0.1	1.0	−0.7	1.6	2.3	0.7	1.9	1.1	1.5	1.6	1.7	3.5	2.9

Source: Authors' calculations.

References

Acharya, V. & Naqvi, H. (2012). The Seeds of a Crisis: A Theory of Bank Liquidity and Risk Taking Over the Business Cycle. *Journal of Financial Economics*, **106**(2), 349–66.

Agoraki, M. E. K., Delis, M. D. & Pasiouras, F. (2011). Regulations, Competition and Bank Risk-Taking in Transition Countries. *Journal of Financial Stability*, **7**(1), 38–48.

Agresti, A. M., Baudino, P. & Poloni, P. (2008). *The ECB and IMF Indicators for the Macro-Prudential Analysis of the Banking Sectors*. ECB Occasional paper series No. 2008–99. https://ideas.repec.org/p/ecb/ecbops/200899.html.

Ahi, K. & Laidroo, L. (2019). Banking Market Competition in Europe – Financial Stability or Fragility Enhancing? *Quantitative Finance and Economics*, **3**(2), 257–285.

Akosah, N., Loloh, F., Lawson, N. & Kumah, C. (2018). *Measuring Financial Stability in Ghana: A New Index-Based Approach*. MPRA Paper No. 86634. https://ideas.repec.org/p/pra/mprapa/86634.html.

Alakbarov, A., Gulaliyev, M., Khudiyev, N. et al. (2018). Financial Stability Assessment of the Banking Sector on the Basis of Composite Index. *Journal of Business and Economic Management*, **6**(1), 1–6.

Albulescu, C. T. (2010). Forecasting the Romanian Financial System Using a Stochastic Simulation Model. *Journal for Economic Forecasting*, **13**(1), 81–98.

Albulescu, C. T. (2013). Financial Stability and Monetary Policy: A Reduced-Form Model for the EURO Area. *Journal for Economic Forecasting*, **16**(1), 62–81.

Allen, F., Jackowicz, K., Kowalewski, O. & Kozłowski, Ł. (2017). Bank Lending, Crises, and Changing Ownership Structure in Central and Eastern European Countries. *Journal of Corporate Finance*, **42**, 494–515.

Al-Rjoub, S. A. M. (2021). A Financial Stability Index for Jordan. *Journal of Central Banking Theory and Practice*, **10**(2), 157–78.

Altan, M., Yusufazari, H. & Bedük, A. (28 October 2014). Performance Analysis of Banks in Turkey Using CAMEL Approach, *Conference Proceedings from 14th International Academic Conference*. International Institute of Social and Economic Sciences. Malta. www.researchgate.net/profile/Habib-Y-Azari/publication/269112160_PERFORMANCE_ANALYSIS_OF_BANKS_IN_TURKEY_USING_CAMEL_APPROACH_INTRODUCTION/links/5481e8600cf2e5f7ceaa8d70/PERFORMANCE-ANALYSIS-OF-BANKS-IN-TURKEY-USING-CAMEL-APPROACH-INTRODUCTION.pdf.

Altman, E. I. (1968). Financial Ratios, Discriminant Analysis and the Prediction of Corporate Failure. *Journal of Finance*, **23**(4), 589–609.

Altman, E. I. (1993). *Corporate Financial Distress and Bankruptcy: A Complete Guide to Predicting and Avoiding Distress and Profiting from Bankruptcy.* 2nd ed. New York: John Wiley.

Altman, E. I. (2000). Predicting *Financial Distress of Companies: Revisiting Z-Score and ZETA Model*s. New York: Stern School of Business, New York University, 9–12.

Ashcraft, A. (2008). Are Bank Holding Companies a Source of Strength to Their Banking Subsidiaries? *Journal of Money, Credit and Banking*, **40**, 273–94.

Audi, M., Kassem, M. & Roussel, J. (2021). Determinants of Banks Fragility in the Mena Region Using a Dynamic Model. *Journal of Developing Areas*, **55**(1), 79–90.

Aytac Emin, A., Dalgic, B. & Azrak, T. (2021). Constructing a Banking Fragility Index for Islamic Banks: Definition Impact on the Predictive Power of an Early Warning System. *Applied Economics Letters*, **28**(18), 1589–93.

Azmi, W., Ali, M., Arshad, S. & Rizvi, S. A. R. (2019). Intricacies of Competition, Stability, and Diversification: Evidence from Dual Banking Economies. *Economic Modelling*, **83**, 111–26.

Baltes, N. & Rodean, C. M. D. (2014). Study Regarding the Financial Stability of Commercial Banks Listed on Bucharest Stock Exchange of CAMELS Rating Outlook. *Journal of International Studies*, **7**(3), 133–43.

Bayar, Y., Borozan, D. & Gavriletea, M. D. (2021). Banking Sector Stability and Economic Growth in Post-transition European Union Countries. *International Journal of Finance & Economics*, **26**(1), 949–61.

Beaver, W. H. (1966). Financial Ratios as Predictors of Failure. *Empirical Research in Accounting: Selected Studies*, **4**, 71–102.

Beck, T. (2008). *Bank Competition and Financial Stability: Friends or Foes?* Policy Research Working Paper Series 4656. Washington DC: The World Bank.

Beck, T., Büyükkarabacak, B., Rioja, F. K. & Valev, N. T. (2012). Who Gets the Credit? And Does It Matter? Household vs. Firm Lending across Countries. *B.E. Journal of Macroeconomics*, **12**(1), 1–46.

Berger, A. N. & Demirgüç-Kunt, A. (2021). Banking Research in the Time of COVID-19. *Journal of Financial Stability*, **57,** 20. https://doi.org/10.1016/j .jfs.2021.100939.

Berger, A. N., Miller, N. H., Petersen, M. A., Rajan, R. G. & Stein, J. C. (2005). Does Function Follow Organizational Form? Evidence from the Lending

Practices of Large and Small Banks. *Journal of Financial Economies*, **76**(2), 237–69.

Berger, A. N., Klapper, L. F. & Turk-Ariss, R. (2009). Bank Competition and Financial Stability. *Journal of Financial Services Research*, **35**(2), 99–118.

Berger, A. N., Cai, J., Roman, R. A. & Sedunov, J. (2022). Supervisory Enforcement Actions against Banks and Systemic Risk. *Journal of Banking & Finance*, **140**, 31.

Berrospide, J. (2013). *Bank Liquidity Hoarding and the Financial Crisis: An Empirical Evaluation*, Finance and Economic Discussion Series of Federal Reserve Board No. 03. www.federalreserve.gov/econres/feds/bank-liquidity-hoarding-and-the-financial-crisis-an-empirical-evaluation.htm.

Bilan, I. & Roman, A. (2016). Macroeconomic Environment and Banking Sector Soundness in CEE Countries. *Ovidius University Annals*, *Economic Sciences Series*, **16**(2), 421–6.

BIS (1995). *The Supervision of Financial Conglomerates*. www.bis.org/publ/bcbs20.htm.

BOA (2010). *Financial Stability Report 2010 H1*. Tirana: Bank of Albania.

Bogetoft, P. & Otto, L. (2011). *Benchmarking with DEA, SFA, and R*. New York: Springer Science and Business Media.

Borgioli, S., Gouveia, A. & Labanca, C. (2013). Financial Stability Analysis: Insights Gained from Consolidated Banking Data for the EU. ECB Occasional Paper No. 140. https://ssrn.com/abstract=2184844.

Boyd, D., Grossman, P., Lankford, H., Loeb, S. & Wyckoff, J. (2006). How Changes in Entry Requirements Alter the Teacher Workforce and Affect Student Achievement. *Education Finance and Policy*, **1**, 176–216.

Boyd, J. H. & Graham, S. L. (1986). Risk, Regulation, and Bank Holding Company Expansion into Nonbanking. *Quarterly Review*, **10**(2), 2–17.

Boyd, J. H. & Graham, S. L. (1988). The Profitability and Risk Effects of Allowing Bank Holding Companies to Merge with Other Financial Firms: A Simulation Study. *Quarterly Review*, **12**, 3–20.

Boyd, J. H., Graham, S. L. & Hewitt, S. R. (1993). Bank Holding Company Mergers with Nonbank Financial Firms: Effects on the Risk of Failure. *Journal of Banking and Finance*, **17**, 43–63.

Brei, M., Gadanecz, B. & Mehrotra, A. (2020). SME Lending and Banking System Stability: Some Mechanisms at Work, *Emerging Markets Review*, **43**(2), 1–11.

Brossard, O., Ducrozet, F. & Roche, A. (2007). An Early Warning Model for EU Banks with Detection of the Adverse Selection Effect. Cahiers du GRES, No. 2007–8.

Buch, C. (2020). *Financial Stability and too-big-to-fail after the Covid-19 Pandemic.* https://www.bls.org/review/r201216c.pdf.

Campello, M. (2002). Internal Capital Markets in Financial Conglomerates: Evidence from Small Bank Responses to Monetary Policy. *The Journal of Finance*, **57**(6), 2773–805.

Capraru, B. & Andries, A. M. (2015). Nexus between Concentration and Fragility across EU Banking Systems. *Procedia Economics and Finance*, **32**, 1140–7.

CBRT (2006). *Financial Stability Report, vol. 2, June 2006.* Ankara: Central Bank of the Republic of Turkey.

Cheang, N. & Choy, I. (2009). *Aggregate Financial Stability Index for an Early Warning System. Macao Monetary Research Bulletin No. 21*, Macau: Monetary Authority of Macao.

Chiaramonte, L., Croci, E. & Poli, F. (2015). Should We Trust the Z-score? Evidence from the European Banking Industry. *Global Finance Journal*, **28**, 111–31.

Chiaramonte, L., Liu, H., Poli, F. & Zhou, M. (2016). How Accurately Can Z-score Predict Bank Failure? *Financial Markets, Institutions and Instruments*, **25**(5), 333–60.

Chiaramonte, L., Dreassi, A., Girardone, C. & Pisera, S. (2021). Do ESG Strategies Enhance Bank Stability During Financial Turmoil? Evidence from Europe. *The European Journal of Finance,* **28**(12), 1173–1211. https://doi.org/10.1080/1351847X.2021.1964556.

Calomiris, C. W., Jaremski, M. & Wheelock, D. C. (2022). Interbank Connections, Contagion and Bank Distress in the Great Depression. *Journal of Financial Intermediation*, **2022**(51), 13.

Chodorow-Reich, G. & Falato, A. (2022). The Loan Covenant Channel: How Bank Health Transmits to the Real Economy. *The Journal of Finance*, **77**(1), 85–128.

Čihák, M. & Hesse, H. (2008). *Islamic Banks and Financial Stability: An Empirical Analysis.* IMF Working Paper No. 08/16. https://ssrn.com/abstract=1089682.

Čihák, M. & Hesse, H. (2010). Islamic Banks and Financial Stability: An Empirical Analysis. *Journal of Financial Services Research*, **38**(2), 95–113.

Čihák, M. (2007). Systemic Loss: A Measure of Financial Stability. *Finance a úvěr – Czech Journal of Economics and Finance*, **57**(1–2), 5–26.

Clark, E., Radić, N. & Sharipova, A. (2018). Bank Competition and Stability in the CIS Markets. *Journal of International Financial Markets, Institutions and Money*, **54**, 190–203.

Clayton, C. & Schaab, A. (2022). Multinational Banks and Financial Stability. *The Quarterly Journal of Economics*, **137**(3), 1681–736.

CNB (2021). *Financial Stability.* www.cnb.cz/en/financial-stability/.

Cornett, M. M., McNutt, J. J., Strahan, P. E. & Tehranian, H. (2012). Liquidity Risk Management and Credit Supply in the Financial Crisis. *Journal of Financial Economics*, **101**(2), 297–312.

Curak, M., Pepur, S. & Poposki, K. (2013). Determinants of Non-performing Loans – Evidence from Southeastern European Banking Systems. *Banks and Bank Systems*, **8**(1), 45–53.

Dages, G., Goldberg, L. & Kinney, D. (2000). Foreign and Domestic Bank Participation in Emerging Markets: Lessons from Mexico and Argentina. *Economic Policy Review*, **6**(3), 17–36.

Danisman, G. O. &Tarazi, A. (2020). Financial Inclusion and Bank Stability: Evidence from Europe. *European Journal of Finance*, **26**(18), 1842–55.

De Haas, R. & Van Lelyveld, I. (2006). Foreign Banks and Credit Stability in Central and Eastern Europe. A Panel Data Analysis. *Journal Bank & Finance*, **30**, 1927–52.

Degl′Innocenti, M., Grant, K., Ševic, A. & Tzeremes, N. (2018). Financial Stability, Competitiveness and Banks′ Innovation Capacity: Evidence from the Global Financial Crisis. *International Review of Financial Analysis*, **59**(C), 35–46.

De Haas, R. & Van Lelyveld, I. (2014). Multinational Banks and the Global Financial Crisis: Weathering the Perfect Storm? *Journal of Money, Credit and Banking*, **46**(s1), 333–64.

Demirgüc-Kunt, A. & Huizinga, H. (2010). Bank Activity and Funding Strategies: The Impact on Risk and Returns. *Journal of Financial Economics*, **98**(3), 626–50.

Didier, T., Huneeus, F. Larrain, M. & Schmukler, S. (2021). Financing Firms in Hibernation during the COVID-19 Pandemic. *Journal of Financial Stability,* **53,** 100837.

Dierick, F. (2004). *The Supervision of Mixed Financial Services Groups in Europe.* ECB Occasional Paper No. 20. https://ideas.repec.org/p/ecb/ecbops/200420.html.

Duan, Y., Ghoul, S. E., Guedhami, O., Li, H. & Li, X. (2021). Bank Systemic Risk around COVID-19: A Cross-Country Analysis. *Journal of Banking and Finance*, **133**, 1–13.

Dumičić, M. (2016). Financial Stability Indicators – The Case of Croatia. *Journal of Central Banking Theory and Practice*, **5**(1), 113–40.

ECB, 2007. *Financial Stability Review, June 2007.* https://www.ecb.europa.eu/pub/pdf/fsr/financialstabilityreview200706en.pdf.

Ellis, S., Sharma, S. & Brzeszczyński, J. (2021). Systemic Risk Measures and Regulatory Challenges. *Journal of Financial Stability*, **6**, 100960.

Fiordelisi, F. & Mare, D. (2014). Competition and Financial Stability in European Cooperative Banks. *Journal of International Money and Finance*, **45**(C), 1–16.

Fiordelisi, F., Marques-Ibanez, D. & Molyneux, P. (2011). Efficiency and Risk in European Banking. *Journal of Banking & Finance*, **35**(5), 1315–26.

Freixas, X., Lóránth, G. & Morrison, A. D. (2007). Regulating Financial Conglomerates. *Journal of Financial Intermediation*, **16**(4), 497–514.

Fu, X. M., Lin, R. Y. & Molyneux, P. (2014). Bank Competition and Financial Stability in Asia Pacific. *Journal of Banking & Finance*, **38**(C), 64–77.

Gadanecz, B. & Jayaram, K. (2009). *Measures of Financial Stability – a Review*. IFC Bulletin No. 31. www.bis.org/ifc/publ/ifcb31ab.pdf.

Gao, J. & Reed, R. R. (2021). Sunspot Bank Runs and Fragility: The Role of Financial Sector Competition. *European Economic Review*, **139**, 37. https://doi:10.1016/j.euroecorev.2021.103877.

Gatzert, N. & Schmeiser, H. (2008). *On the Risk Situation of Financial Conglomerates: Does Diversification Matter?* Working Papers on Risk Management and Insurance No. 50. www.ivw.unisg.ch/~/media/internet/content/dateien/instituteundcenters/ivw/wps/wp50.pdf.

Geršl, A. & Heřmánek, J. (2008). Indicators of Financial System Stability: Towards and Aggregate Financial Stability Indicator. *Prague Economic Papers*, **17**(2), 127–42.

Gilbert, R. A., Meyer, A. P. & Vaughan, M. D. (2000). *The Role of a CAMEL Downgrade Model in Bank Surveillance*. Federal Reserve Bank of St. Louis Working Paper Series, No. 2000-021A.

Ginevičius, R. & Podviezko, A. (2013). The Evaluation of Financial Stability and Soundness of Lithuanian Banks. *Ekonomska Istraživanja*, **26**(2), 191–208.

Godlewski, C. (2005). Bank Capital and Credit Risk Taking in Emerging Market Economies. *Journal of Banking Regulation*, **6**, 128–45.

Goetz, M. R., Laeven, L. & Levine, R. (2016). Does the Geographic Expansion of Banks Reduce Risk? *Journal of Financial Economics*, **120**(2), 346–62.

Gospodarchuk, G. & Amosova, N. (2020). Geo-financial Stability of the Global Banking System. *Banks and Bank Systems*, **15**(4), 164–78.

Greenwood, R., Hanson, S. G., Shleifer, A. & Sorensen, J. A. (2022). Predictable Financial Crises. *The Journal of Finance*, **77**(2), 863–921.

Gulaliyev M. G., Ashurbayli-Huseynova N. P., Gubadova A. A. et al. (2019). Stability of the Banking Sector: Deriving Stability Indicators and Stress-testing. *Polish Journal of Management Studies*, **19**(2), 182–95.

Hassan, M. K. & Miah, M. D. (2022). *Banking Sector Reforms: Is China Following Japan's Footstep?* (Elements in the Economics of Emerging Markets). Cambridge: Cambridge University Press.

Hays, F., De Lurgio, S. & Gilbert, A. J. (2009). Efficiency Ratios and Community Bank Performance. *Journal of Finance and Accountancy*, **1**(1), 1–15.

Herring, R. (2003). International Financial Conglomerates: Implications for Bank Insolvency Regimes. *Market Discipline in Banking: Theory and Evidence*, **15**, 99–129.

Herring, R. & Carmassi, J. (2012) The Corporate Structure of International Financial Conglomerates. In Berger, A. N., Molyneux, P. Wilson, J. O. S. (eds.) *The Oxford Handbook of Banking*. Oxford: Oxford University Press, 195–230.

Hesse, M. H. & Čihák, M. (2007). *Cooperative Banks and Financial Stability.* IMF Working Paper No. 2007–2. www.elibrary.imf.org/view/journals/001/2007/002/article-A001-en.xml.

Horváth, R. (2009). *Interest Margins Determinants of Czech Banks*. Working Paper of the Instsitute of Economic Studies of the Charles University No. 11/09. https://ideas.repec.org/a/fau/fauart/v59y2009i2p128-136.html.

Huljak, I. (2015). Market Power and Stability of CEE Banks. *Business Systems Research*, **6**(2), 74–90.

Iannotta, G., Nocera, G. & Sironi, A. (2007). Ownership Structure, Risk and Performance in the European Banking Industry. *Journal of Banking & Finance*, **31**(7), 2127–49.

ICA (2020). *How strong are your CAMELS?* www.int-comp.org/insight/2020/february/04/camels-analysis/.

Ijaz, S., Hassan, A., Tarazi, A. & Fraz, A. (2020). Linking Bank Competition, Financial Stability, and Economic Growth. *Journal of Business Economics and Management*, **21**(1), 200–21.

Illing, M. & Liu, Y. (2003). *An Index of Financial Stress for Canada*. Bank of Canada. Working Paper No. 2003–14. www.bankofcanada.ca/2003/06/working-paper-2003-14/.

IMF (2005). *Chapter 3: Assessing Financial Stability.* www.elibrary.imf.org/view/books/069/02403-9780821364321-en/ch03.xml.

IMF (2006). *Financial Soundness Indicators. Compilation Guide.* www.imf.org/external/pubs/ft/fsi/guide/2006/pdf/fsiFT.pdf.

IMF (2019). *Financial Soundness Indicators (FSIs).* https://data.imf.org/?sk=51B096FA-2CD2-40C2-8D09-0699CC1764DA.

IMF (2021). *Financial System Soundness.* www.imf.org/en/About/Factsheets/Financial-System-Soundness.

Inanoglu H., Jacobs, M., Liu, J. & Sickles, R. (2016). Analyzing Bank Efficiency: Are 'Too-Big-to-Fail' Banks Efficient? In Haven E., Molyneux P., Wilson J. O. S., Fedotov S. & Duygun, M. (eds.) *The Handbook of Post Crisis Financial Modeling*. London: Palgrave Macmillan, 110–46.

Ivicic, L., Kunovac, D. & Ljubaj, I. (2008). *Measuring bank insolvency risk in CEE countries*. The Fourteenth Dubrovnik Economic Conference. www.hnb.hr›ivicic-kunovac-ljubaj-3.pdf.

Jakubík, P. & Slačík, T. (2013). *Measuring Financial (In)Stability in Emerging Europe: A New Index-Based Approach*. Financial Stability Report of Oesterreihische Nationalbank, pp. 102–17. https://ideas.repec.org/a/onb/oenbfs/y2013i25b5.html.

Joint Forum (1999). *Capital Adequacy Principles Paper*. www.bis.org/publ/bcbs47ch2.pdf.

Jokipii, T. & Milne, A. (2008). The Cyclical Behaviour of European Bank Capital Buffers. *Journal of Banking and Finance*, **32**(8), 1440–51.

Kaffash, S., Matin, R. K. & Mohammad Tajik, M. (2018). A Directional Semi-oriented Radial DEA Measure: An Application on Financial Stability and the Efficiency of Banks. *Annals of Operations Research*, **264**(1–2), 213–34.

Karanovic, G. & Karanovic, B. (2015). Developing an Aggregate Index for Measuring Financial Stability in the Balkans. *Procedia Economics and Finance*, **2015**(33), 3–17.

Karim, N. A., Alhabshi, S. M. S. J., Kassim, S. & Haron, R. (2019). Critical Review of Bank Stability Measures in Selected Countries with Dual Banking System. *Revista Publicando*, **6**(19), 118–31.

Karkowska, R. & Pawlowska, M. (2017). *The Concentration and Bank Stability in Central and Eastern European countries*. Working Paper of Narodowy Bank Polski, 272–2017. https://ideas.repec.org/p/nbp/nbpmis/272.html.

Kim, H., Batten, J. A. & Ryu, D. (2020). Financial Crisis, Bank Diversification, and Financial Stability: OECD countries. *International Review of Economics and Finance*, **65**, 94–104.

Klepková Vodová, P. (2018). Effects of Affiliation with the Financial Conglomerate on Bank Liquidity and Solvency in the Visegrad Countries. *Acta Academica Karviniensia*, **18**(2), 16–25.

Klepková Vodová, P. (2019). Determinants of Solvency in Selected CEE Banking Sectors: Does Affiliation with the Financial Conglomerate Matter? *Acta Universitatis Agriculturae et Silviculturae Mendeleianae Brunensis*, **67**(2), 493–501.

Kočišová, K. (2015). Banking Stability Index: A Cross-Country Study. In Palečková, I. & Szarowska, I. (eds.) *Proceedings of the 15th International Conference on Finance and Banking*. Karviná: Silesian University, 197–208.

Kočišová, K. (2020). Competition and Stability in the European Global Systemically Important Banks. *Ekonomický časopis*, **68**(5), 431–54.

Kočišová, K., Gavurova, B. & Behun, M. (2018). The Evaluation of Stability of Czech and Slovak Banks. *Oeconomia Copernicana*, **9**(2), 205–23.

Kočišová, K. & Stavárek, D. (2015). *Banking Stability Index: New EU countries after Ten Years of Membership*, No 0024, Working Papers, Silesian University, School of Business Administration.

Kočišová, K. & Stavárek, D. (2018). The Evaluation of Banking Stability in the European Union Countries. *International Journal of Monetary Economics and Finance*, **11**(1), 36–55.

Kondratovs, K. (2014). Modelling Financial Stability Index for Latvian Financial System. *Regional Formation and Development Studies*, **8**(3), 118–29.

König-Kersting, C., Trautmann, S. T. & Vlahu, R. (2022). Bank Instability: Interbank Linkages and the Role of Disclosure. *Journal of Banking & Finance*, **2022**(134), 17.

Krug, S., Lengnick, M. & Wohltmann, H. W. (2015). The Impact of Basel III on Financial (In)stability – An Agent-based Credit Network Approach. *Quantitative Finance*, **15**(12), 1917–32.

Kwan, S. & Eisenbeis, R. A. (1997). Bank Risk, Capitalization, and Operating Efficiency. *Journal of Financial Services Research*, **12**(2), 117–31.

Laeven, L. & Levine, R. (2007). Is There a Diversification Discount in Financial Conglomerates? *Journal of Financial Economics*, **85**(2), 331–67.

Laeven, L. & Levine, R. (2009). Bank Governance, Regulation and Risk Taking. *Journal of Financial Econometrics*, **93**(2), 259–75.

Lapteacru, I. (2016). *On the Consistency of the Z-Score to Measure the Bank Risk*. https://ssrn.com/abstract=2787567.

Laznia, M. (2013). *Kde nájdeme najstabilnejšie banky*? www.sbaonline.sk/sk/presscentrum/aktuality/tema-kde-najdeme-najstabilnejsie-banky.html.

Lepetit, L. & Strobel, F. (2015). Bank Insolvency Risk and Z-Score Measures: A Refinement. *Finance Research Letters*, **13**, 214–24.

Lepetit, L., Nys, E., Rous, P. & Tarazi, A. (2008). Bank Income Structure and Risk: An Empirical Analysis of European Banks. *Journal of Banking and Finance*, **32**(8), 1452–67.

Leroy, A. & Lucotte, Y. (2017). Is There a Competition-stability Trade-off in European Banking? *Journal of International Financial Markets, Institutions and Money*, **46**(C), 199–215.

Lindgren, C. J. & Folkerts-Landau, D. F. I. (1998). Toward a Framework for Financial Stability. World Economic and Financial Surveys. International Monetary Fund. www.elibrary.imf.org/view/books/083/07429-97815577570 67-en/07429-9781557757067-en-book.xml?BookTabs=BookTOC.

Lucchetta, M. (2007). What Do Data Say about Monetary Policy, Bank Liquidity and Bank Risk Taking? *Economic Notes by Banca Monte dei Paschi di Siena SpA*, **36**(2), 189–203.

Lukić, V., Popović, S. & Janković, I. (2019). Nonperforming Loans and Financial Stability – The Case of Serbia. *Facta Universitatis, Series: Economics and Organization*, **16**(4), 349–64.

Maishanu, M. (2004). A Univariate Approach to Predicting Failure in the Commercial Banking Sub-Sector in Nigerian. *Journal of Accounting Research*, **1**(1), 70–84.

Mälkönen, V. (2009). Financial Conglomeration and Monitoring Incentives. *Journal of Financial Stability*, **5**(2), 105–23.

Massa, M. & Rehman, Z. (2008). Information Flows Within Financial Conglomerates: Evidence From the Banks–mutual Funds Relation. *Journal of Financial Economics*, **89**(2), 288–306.

Ma Mateev, M., Tariq, M. U. & Sahyouni, A. (2021). Competition, Capital Growth and Risk-taking in Emerging Markets: Policy Implications for Banking Sector Stability during COVID-19 Pandemic. *PLoS One*, **16**(6), 1–36.

Matousek, R. & Rummel, O. (2020). *Cross-Border Interbank Contagion Risk Analysis. Evidence from Selected Emerging and Less-developed Economies in the Asia-Pacific Region*. (Elements in the Economics of Emerging Markets). Cambridge: Cambridge University Press.

Maudos, J. (2012). Financial Soundness Indicators for the Spanish Banking Sector: An International Comparison. *SEFO-Spanish Economic and Financial Outlook*, **1**(4), 24–32.

Mercieca, S., Schaeck, K. & Wolfe, S. (2007). Small European Banks: Benefits from Diversification? *Journal of Banking and Finance*, **31**, 1975–98.

Miklaszewska, E., Mikolajczyk, K. & Pawlowska, M. (2012). *The consequences of post-crisis regulatory architecture for banks in Central Eastern Europe*. National Bank of Poland Working Paper No. 131. https://papers.ssrn.com/sol3/papers.cfm?abstract_id=2190850.

Minh, S. N., Hong, V. N. T., Hoang, L. L. & Thuy, T. N. T. (2020). Does Banking Market Power Matter on Financial Stability? *Management Science Letters*, **10**(2), 343–50.

Minsky, H. P. (1977). The Financial Instability Hypothesis: An Interpretation of Keynes and an Alternative to 'Standard' Theory. *Challenge*, **20**(1), 20–7.

Mishkin, F. S. (1990). *Asymmetric Information and Financial Crises: A Historical Perspective*. NBER Working Paper No. 3400. www.nber.org/papers/w3400.

Mishra, R. N., Majumdar, S. & Bhandia, D. (2013). *Banking Stability – A Precursor to Financial Stability*. Working Paper Series No. 2013-01. www.rbi.org.in/Scripts/PublicationsView.aspx?id=14916.

Morris, V. C. (2011). Measuring and Forecasting Financial Stability: The Composition of an Aggregate Financial Stability Index for Jamaica. Business, *Finance & Economics in Emerging Economies*, **6**(2), 34–51.

Mörttinen, L., Poloni, P., Sandars, P. & Vesala, J. (2005). *Analysing Banking Sector Conditions: How to Use Macro-prudential Indicators*. ECB Occasional Paper Series No. 26. https://ideas.repec.org/p/ecb/ecbops/200526.html.

Natalya, M., Ratnovski, L. & Vlahu, R. (2015). *Bank Profitability and Risk-Taking*. IMF Working Paper No. 15/249. www.imf.org/en/Publications/WP/Issues/2016/12/31/Bank-Profitability-and-Risk-Taking-43421.

Nelson, W. R. & Perli, R. (2007). *Selected Indicators of Financial Stability*. In *ECB. Risk Measurement and Systemic Risk*. Frankfurt am Main: European Central Bank, 343–72. www.ecb.europa.eu/pub/pdf/other/riskmeasurementandsystemicrisk200704en.pdf

OECD (2008). *Handbook on Constructing Composite Indicators. Methodology and User Guide*. Paris: OECD.

Palečková, I. (2018). *Performance Measurement in Banking: Empirical Application to Central and Eastern Europe*. Praha: Professional.

Park, C. Y. & Shin, M. M. (2021). COVID-19, Nonperforming Loans, and Cross-border Bank Lending. *Journal of Banking and Finance*, **133**, 1–14.

Pavković, A., Cesarec, A. & Stojanović, A. (2018). Profitability and Efficiency of the Croatian Banking Sector: Impact of Bank Size. *International Journal of Trade and Global Markets*, **22**(4), 243–58.

Peleckiene, V., Peleckis, K. & Dudzeviciute, G. (2011). New Challenges of Supervising Financial Conglomerates. *Intelektine ekonomika*, **5**(20), 298–311.

Petrovska, M. & Mihajlovska, E. M. (2013). Measures of Financial Stability in Macedonia. *Journal of Central Banking Theory and Practice*, **2**(3), 85–110.

Pietrzak, M. (2021). *Can Financial Soundness Indicators Help Predict Financial Sector Distress?* IMF Working Paper no. WP/21/197. www.imf.org/-/media/Files/Publications/WP/2021/English/wpiea2021197-print-pdf.ashx.

Popovska, J. (2014). Modelling Financial Stability: The Case of the Banking Sector in Macedonia. *Journal of Applied Economics and Business*, **2**(1), 68–91.

Raykov, R. S. & Silva-Buston, C. (2020). Holding Company Affiliation and Bank Stability: Evidence from the US Banking Sector. *Journal of Corporate Finance*, **65**, 1–24.

Roman, A. & Sargu, A. C. (2013). Analysing the Financial Soundness of the Commercial Banks in Romania: An Approach Based on the Camels Framework. *Procedia Economics and Finance*, **6**, 703–12.

Salas, V. & Saurina, J. (2002). Credit Risk in Two Institutional Regimes: Spanish Commercial and Savings Banks. *Journal of Financial Services Research*, **22**(3), 203–24.

Şargu, A. C. & Roman, A. (2013). A Cross-Country Analysis of the Banks' Financial Soundness: The Case of the CEE-3 Countries. *Annals of Faculty of Economics* **1**(1), 357–67.

Schaeck, K. & Čihák, M. (2014). Competition, Efficiency, and Stability in Banking. *Financial Management*, **43**(1), 215–41.

Schinasi, G. J. (2004). *Defining Financial Stability*. IMF Working Paper No. 04/187. www.elibrary.imf.org/view/journals/001/2004/187/article-A001-en.xml.

Schmid, M. M. & Walter, I. (2009). Do Financial Conglomerates Create or Destroy Economic Value? *Journal of Financial Intermediation*, **18**(2), 193–216.

Schuknecht, L. (2022). *Debt Sustainability. A Global Perspective.* (Cambridge Elements in International Economics). Cambridge: Cambridge University Press.

Shaddady, A. & Moore, T. (2019). Investigation of the Effects of Financial Regulation and Supervision on Bank Stability: The Application of CAMELS-DEA to Quantile Regressions. *Journal of International Financial Markets, Institutions and Money*, **58**, 96–116.

Shahzad, A., Hussain, H., Ismail, H. & Ullah, M. I. (2020). Bank Stability Index Determinants: A PCA Approach. *Pakistan Journal of Social Sciences*, **40**(2), 983–94.

Shijaku, G. (2017). Bank Stability and Competition: Evidence from Albanian Banking Market. *Eurasian Journal of Business and Economics*, **19**(10), 127–54.

SNB (2006). *Financial Stability Report, June 2006*. Zurich: Swiss National Bank.

Sprague, O. M. W. (1910). *History of Crises under the National Banking System*. National Monetary Commission. Washington, DC: U.S. Government Printing Office.

Staikouras, C. & Wood, G. E. (2004). The Determinants of European Bank Profitability. *International Journal of Economics and Business Research*, **3**(6), 57–68.

Stolz, S. & Wedow, M. (2011). Banks´ Regulatory Capital Buffer and the Business Cycle: Evidence for Germany. *Journal of Financial Stability*, **7**(2), 98–110.

Šubová, N. & Kočišová, K. (2019). Market Power, Stability and Bank Profitability: Evidence from Slovakia. *Acta Oeconomica Universitatis Selye*, **8**(1), 176–86.

Supangkat, T., Sofilda, E., Hamzah, M. Z. & Ginting, A. M. (2020). The Impact of Financial and Competition Conglomeration Policies on Banking Efficiency and Risk in Indonesia. *Banks and Bank System*, **15**(3), 29–43.

Todorović, V., Furtula, S. & Durkalić, D. (2018). Measuring Performance of the Serbian Banking Sector Using CAMELS Model. *TEME*, **42**(3), 961–77.

Uhde, A. & Heimeshoff, U. (2009). Consolidation in Banking and Financial Stability in Europe: Empirical Evidence. *Journal of Banking & Finance*, **33**, 1299–311.

Van den End, J. W. & Tabbae, M. (2005). *Measuring Financial Stability: Applying the MfRisk Model to the Netherlands*. De Nederlandsche Bank Working Paper No. 2005-30. https://ideas.repec.org/p/dnb/dnbwpp/030.html.

Van den End, J. W. (2006). *Indicator and Boundaries of Financial Stability*. De Nederlandsche Bank Working Paper No. 2006–97. https://ideas.repec.org/p/dnb/dnbwpp/097.html.

Vander Vennet, R. (2002). Cost and Profit Efficiency of Financial Conglomerates and Universal Banks in Europe. *Journal of Money, Credit, and Banking*, **34**(1), 254–282.

Vesala, J., Poloni, P., Mörttinen, L. & Sandars, P. (2005). Analysing Banking Sector Conditions – How to Use Macro-Prudential Indicators. *Occasional Paper Series*, 26, European Central Bank.

Vodová, P. (2013). *Liquidity Risk of Banks in the Visegrad Countries: An Empirical Analysis of Bank Liquidity, Its Determinants and Liquidity Risk Sensitivity*. Saarbrücken: Lambert Academic.

World Bank (2018). *Romania Financial Sector Assessment Program: Financial Intermediation*. Washington: World Bank.

World Bank (2021). Financial Stability. www.worldbank.org/en/publication/gfdr/gfdr-2016/background/financial-stability.

Wu, J., Chen, M., Jeon, B. N. & Wang, R. (2017). Does Foreign Bank Penetration Affect the Risk of Domestic Banks? Evidence from Emerging Economies. *Journal of Financial Stability*, **31**, 45–61.

Zhang, J. (2019). Stability and Risk of Financial Holding Companies – Taking the Chinese CITIC Group as Example. *Journal of Service Science and Management*, **12**(2), 246–66.

Zigraiova, D. & Havranek, T. (2016). Bank Competition and Financial Stability: Much Ado about Nothing? *Journal of Economic Surveys*, **30**(5), 944–81.

Legislative Documents:

Commission Delegated Regulation (EU) no 342/2014 of 21 January 2014 supplementing Directive 2002/87/EC of the European Parliament and of the Council and Regulation (EU) No 575/2013 of the European Parliament and of the Council with regard to regulatory technical standards for the application of the calculation methods of capital adequacy requirements for financial conglomerates. https://eur-lex.europa.eu/legal-content/EN/TXT/?uri=CELEX:32014R0342.

Directive 2002/87/EC of the European Parliament and of the Council of 16 December 2002 on the supplementary supervision of credit institutions, insurance undertakings and investment firms in a financial conglomerate and amending Council Directives 73/239/EEC, 79/267/EEC, 92/49/EEC, 92/96/EEC, 93/6/EEC and 93/22/EEC, and Directives 98/78/EC and 2000/12/EC of the European Parliament and of the Council. https://eur-lex.europa.eu/legal-content/en/TXT/?uri=CELEX:32002L0087.

Directive 2011/89/EU of the European Parliament and of the Council of 16 November 2011 amending Directives 98/78/EC, 2002/87/EC, 2006/48/EC and 2009/138/EC as regards the supplementary supervision of financial entities in a financial conglomerate. https://eur-lex.europa.eu/legal-content/EN/TXT/?uri=celex%3A32011L0089

Acknowledgements

This Element was supported by the Ministry of Education, Youth and Sports Czech Republic within the Institutional Support for Long-term Development of a Research Organization in 2021. The support is gratefully acknowledged.

Cambridge Elements ≡

Economics of Emerging Markets

Bruno S. Sergi
Harvard University

Editor Bruno S. Sergi is an instructor at Harvard University, an associate of the Harvard University Davis Center for Russian and Eurasian Studies and Harvard Ukrainian Research Institute. He is the Academic Series Editor of the Cambridge *Elements in the Economics of Emerging Markets* (Cambridge University Press), a co-editor of the *Lab for Entrepreneurship and Development* book series, and an associate editor of *The American Economist*. Concurrently, he teaches International Economics at the University of Messina, Scientific Director of the Lab for Entrepreneurship and Development (LEAD), and is co-founder and Scientific Director of the International Center for Emerging Markets Research at RUDN University in Moscow. He has published over 150 articles in professional journals and twenty-one books as author, co-author, editor, and co-editor.

About the Series

The aim of this Elements series is to deliver state-of-the-art, comprehensive coverage of the knowledge developed to date, including the dynamics and prospects of these economies, focusing on emerging markets' economics, finance, banking, technology advances, trade, demographic challenges, and their economic relations with the rest of the world, as well as the causal factors and limits of economic policy in these markets.

Cambridge Elements ⁝

Economics of Emerging Markets